STOCK MARKET INVESTING

& DAY, SWING AND FOREX

FOR BEGINNERS

Table of Contents

BOOK 1

INTRODUCTION..7

CHAPTER 1. THE BASICS OF INVESTING IN STOCKS.......................14

CHAPTER 2. STEPS TO EVALUATE YOUR FINANCIAL HEALTH, SETTING, GOALS (WHAT TO CONSIDER BEFORE OPENING A NEW ACCOUNT).........................24

CHAPTER 3. RISKS IN INVESTING IN STOCKS..................................32

CHAPTER 4. HOW TO INVEST IN STOCKS (HOW TO BUY YOUR FIRST STOCK) 40

CHAPTER 5. WHEN TO BUY..48

AND SELL STOCK..48

CHAPTER 6. HOW TO GENERATE PASSIVE INCOME FROM THE STOCK MARKET...58

CHAPTER 7. THE MAIN MISTAKES OF A BEGINNER........................64

CHAPTER 8. INSIDER TRICKS USED BY PROFESSIONAL TRADERS...70

CHAPTER 9. TIPS AND TRICKS FOR SUCCESSFUL STOCKS TRADING...78

CHAPTER 10. ADVICE TO MINIMIZING LOSSES AND MAXIMIZING GAINS....86

CHAPTER 11. TAX IMPLICATION AND HOW TO REDUCE THEIR IMPACT ON YOUR EARNINGS...92

CHAPTER 12. WHAT TO DO AND WHAT TO BUY IN A DOWN MARKET......102

CHAPTER 13. HOW TO USE BOTH MACROECONOMIC AND MICROECONOMIC ANALYSIS...110

CHAPTER 14. HOW TO CREATE A SECURE FINANCIAL FUTURE...................116

CHAPTER 15. STOCK MARKET STRATEGIES FOR PROFITABLE INVESTING...128

CHAPTER 16. COVID-19 EFFECTS ON WORKING WITH STOCKS...................132

CONCLUSION..138

BOOK 2

INTRODUCTION 141

CHAPTER 1: DAY TRADING 147

CHAPTER 2: CONSERVATIVE STRATEGY OF DAY TRADING 154

CHAPTER 3: ADVANCED STRATEGY OF DAY TRADING 159

CHAPTER 4: TYPICAL BEGINNER'S ERRORS IN DAY TRADING 167

CHAPTER 5: SWING TRADING 175

CHAPTER 6: CONSERVATIVE STRATEGY OF SWING TRADING 186

CHAPTER 7: ADVANCED STRATEGY OF SWING TRADING 192

CHAPTER 8: TYPICAL BEGINNER'S ERRORS IN SWING TRADING 199

CHAPTER 9: FOREX TRADING 210

CHAPTER 10: CONSERVATIVE STRATEGY FOR FOREX TRADING 216

CHAPTER 11: ADVANCED STRATEGY FOR FOREX TRADING 226

CHAPTER 12: TYPICAL BEGINNER'S ERRORS IN FOREX TRADING 232

CONCLUSION 240

BOOK 3

NFT & METAVERSE (BONUS) 247

STOCK MARKET INVESTING

A Crash Course Guide to Trading from Beginners to Expert:
How to Create Passive Income to Get Fresh Money to Buy and Sell Options

Anthony Sinclair

Introduction

The fact is that for most young people, investing might not be the most important thing in their lives. Until they get older and established in a career, saving and investing for retirement may not be at the top of their priority list; there are other things that might seem more pressing and exciting at this stage in life.

When you're young, you have limited resources to invest. You're also still trying to figure out who you are — what kind of career or education you want to pursue, and how much risk you want to take with your money. For these reasons, it's not a good idea to jump into the stock market before you have a better handle on your financial circumstances and goals.

This doesn't mean you'll never be able to invest in the stock market, but it does mean that you're a long way off from making a decision that will have a major impact on your life. Until then, there are plenty of other ways to get started with investing and he stock market without getting ahead of yourself.

It is difficult to believe there was a time when the stock market didn't exist. The stock market is on the tip of nearly everyone's tongue. Even individuals who do not invest at least know it exists. It is largely understood that the New York Stock Exchange is the biggest market of them all, with any company listed on it that wants to be recognized globally. However, how did the stock market come to fruition? Is there more than the NYSE (New York Stock Exchange)? There are more exchanges and it started with the Real Merchants of Venice and British Coffeehouses.

Europe was filled with moneylenders that filled in the gaps of the larger banks. Moneylenders would trade between themselves. One lender might get rid of a high-risk, high-interest loan by trading it to another lender. Moneylenders also purchased government debt. In a natural evolution, lenders started selling debts to customers who were looking to invest.

Investors also put their money into ships and crews. Most of the time-limited liability companies would go on a single voyage to gain merchandise from Asia and the East Indies as a way to bring a profit to the investor. New companies were usually formed for the next voyage to reduce the risk of investing in ships that could end up in disaster. The East India companies worked with investors by providing dividends made from the goods that came in. Stocks were now in place, where the first joint-stock company was created. At the time, there were royal charters that made competition impossible and thus, investors gained huge profits.

It was not without its troubles. The stock market is based on economic stability. When instability reigns the stock market can crash because there is no liquidity, which is what happened during the Great Depression. Everyone saw the banks failing due to debts and little liquidity, which in turn caused others to suffer, businesses too close, and stock shares to plummet.

The stock market formed from a need to have a place to conduct the business of selling shares, which was already happening. Governments needed to regulate stock sales, and prevent issues like the SSC crash. Nevertheless, there was also greed on behalf of wealthy citizens. There was a clear way to earn money from someone else's labor, thus the stock exchanges were started.

Investors and traders sell stocks after the IPO based on the perceived value. A company's value can go up or down, which is where investors make their money. A company's stock price that rises can provide a profit. If an investor has purchased those shares and the price or company value decreases, then the investor will lose money. In addition, the investors and traders will push the price in an up or down direction.

Investors have one of two goals: investing in the short or the long term. A long-term investment is based on a stock continuing to rise in price. A short-term investment is to gain quick cash and pulling out before the stock price decreases.

Mature companies offer dividends to their shareholders. If you have stocks, then you are a shareholder in a company. If you hold the stocks long enough and have enough stock in a company, you can vote on new board members. Dividends are company profits that you get a cut of.

Investors will make money on the price fluctuations and the dividends. A seller is often trying to gain a profit by selling to a new buyer. The new buyer is also trying to buy as low as possible so that when the stock price continues to increase, they will make a profit.

The profit is calculated by taking the initial buy price and subtracting it from the closing or sale price. For example, if you buy into Google at $400 and wait for it to go up to $600, then the profit is $200 per share.

Sellers can push the price down due to supply and demand. This financial market works based on supply and demand.

You should already know that in economics when there is an oversupply of a product, the price is low. There is no demand for the product; therefore, a company or in this case a stock is not of interest.

When there is an undersupply of something like a stock, the demand is high. With more interested parties, the price will continue to increase.

If there is an even amount of supply and demand, then equality exists and there is no movement to see.

For the stock market, when too many people sell a stock, the price will decline. When too many people buy a stock, the price will continue to rise. If there is an equal number of shares and interest, then the price usually trades sideways because there is a balance.

As you learn about the stock market, you will hear the word volume, often. Volume is the number of shares that change hands on a daily basis. Millions of shares can be traded on the stock exchange in a day as investors attempt to make money from increasing or decreasing prices.

The stock market works based on the interest or volume of traders. If a stock does not have any volume or very little, then it is not being actively traded, thus the price is not moving. Traders such as market makers get into the market in order to buy or sell stocks for companies with low volume. They do not stop a stock from rising or falling. Instead, market makers just trying to garner interest in the company's stock.

When it comes to the stock market and traders, most individuals are looking for high-volume traders, with fluctuating prices. They get in, make a profit, and get out finding the next big profit.

Chapter 1. The Basics of Investing in Stocks

Delayed gratification is a strong suit that few have and this is why investing has always been a challenge for many. You want to make money but not in a decade or a couple of years, but right now. Ponzi schemes aside, profitable investments that can actually build you wealth for a lifetime take time and lots of patience. These two things are probably the most important tools that any beginner in stock market investing needs to be aware of.

Our motivations for investing may differ but ultimately all investments have one goal in common; to make a return or profit on the investment. You may be eyeing early retirement, you may be in it for financial freedom or maybe you are just sick of having your money sitting in a savings account attracting point nothing interest. Regardless of what your goals are, the idea behind investing is that you use your money to make more money.

The stock market presents a unique opportunity for both retail and corporate investors because anyone can do it at any scale. You can invest as little as $1000 or as much as a million dollars. There are room and opportunity for everyone to get in and make a decent return on their investment. That said, the stock market is not the way to go if you want quick money. Stocks like most other investments have one thing in common; they depend on the power of time.

Time is your biggest ally when it comes to investing. If you have been waiting for a magical moment when you will have "enough" money to start investing, the bad news is that you will probably never have "enough" money and the other bad news is that the right time to start investing was yesterday.

A common misconception that most people have is that you need to have a lot of money to start investing. In actual fact, people who invest do not necessarily have more money than you, they simply make investing a priority. And because they make investing a priority, they end up having more money than you. See how that works?

Unlike consumption, investment takes money out of your pocket and puts it towards your future. When you can think of investment as an insurance policy to safeguard your financial future then the decision on when and if to invest becomes pretty much a no-brainer. Nobody wants to be cash-strapped forever or have to work themselves to the grave because they did not put their money to work when they had the chance.

The beauty of this golden age of technology that we live in is that anyone with the will and determination to do so can access all the tools they need to start investing in the stock market. This ease of accessibility coupled with its affordability has made the stock market increasingly popular with retail investors. With just a few a hundred dollars you can find an online brokerage at the click of a button and get started as an investor in the stock market. Yes, it is that easy. Before you jump on the bandwagon, however, it is important to understand what you are investing in. The natural starting point is, of course, understanding how the stock market works.

How Does the Stock Market Work?

It is no coincidence that most people who have wealth have a big part of this wealth invested in stocks. Stocks carry their fair share of risks for any investor but when done right, stock market investing can be one of the most efficient ways to build and retain wealth.

A stock market is an exchange where people trade by buying and selling shares on traded companies. Once you have bought shares in a company your stock gives you ownership of a small part of that company. With this ownership, the value of your investment will be determined by the movements of the price of the company's shares. If for instance, you bought Apple stocks and the price moves up while you are holding the stock then the value of your investment increases. On the other hand, if the price of the Apple stocks decreases while you are holding the stocks, the value of your investment decreases.

The price of a stock is driven by the forces of supply and demand. Naturally, when the demand for a particular stock is higher than the supply, the price of that stock will increase. In much the same way, when the supply is higher than the demand, then the price of that stock will decrease. In essence, the stock price is a reflection of the value as set by the market conditions. When you buy a stock as an investor, your general goal is to make money when the price of the stock increases. This is why a big part of investing in the stock market is knowing how to select the right stocks to buy.

When the price of the shares you have appreciates, you can sell your shares at a profit. This means that you will get a return on your investment and you can reinvest your capital back into the market or you can cash out. The beauty of stock market investing is that there is usually no limit to how long you can hold your investment. You can keep your shares for 20 years or you can choose to sell them when the share price appreciates. This will ultimately depend on what your end goal is.

Price appreciation is not the only way to make money in the stock market. Dividends are payments made out to shareholders when a company makes a profit. This means that depending on the type of shares you have, you will receive dividends from the company whose shares you hold.

For instance, if you bought Tesla stocks and the company pays out dividends quarterly to their shareholders, you will get a percentage of these dividends based on the value of your shares. You can choose to take these dividends as a cash payment or you can choose to reinvest them back into the company by buying more shares.

It is important to note that not all companies pay dividends. This means that if you want to make money in the stock market by earning regular dividends, you will need to understand the type of stocks to buy and which company's stocks will get you dividends.

Stock exchanges like the NYSE (New York Stock Exchange), NASDAQ, the Tokyo Stock Exchange are some of the largest exchanges. However, stocks are also sold in over-the-counter markets where they trade directly through brokers and not in open exchanges like the NYSE. These markets are referred to as secondary markets where investors trade stocks by buying and selling amongst themselves.

Basic Terms and Concepts

- **Stocks**

    A stock is a share of ownership in a company. Stocks are also referred to as shares. When you buy a stock you acquire a fraction of ownership of the company whose shares you have bought. When you buy stocks, you become a shareholder in a particular company and the percentage or size of your shares will determine the dividends you can earn.

Investors in the stock market can make money from their stocks in different ways. You can earn money in the form of dividends paid out on the shares you own. You can also earn money by selling your shares or stocks.

- **Common Stock**

Common stocks give you ownership of a company based on the number of shares you own. Common stocks are the most basic type of shares to own and they entitle you to dividends where applicable and voting rates proportionate to the shares you own.

- **Preferred Stock**

Preferred stocks entitle you to a fixed dividend rate for your shares. With this type of stock, you earn dividends before shareholders who have common stock but you do not get voting rights. Unlike shareholders of common stocks, preferred stocks give you a guarantee that you will receive dividends on your stock.

- **Penny Stocks**

A penny stock is a stock that trades for less than $5 per share. Penny stocks are typically short-term holdings where you want to take advantage of price movements in volatile markets. Penny stocks investing works for short-term investors who do not plan to hold the stocks for long periods.

- **Blue Chip Stocks**

Blue-chip stocks are shares of large established corporations that have solid reputations in the market. Blue-chip stocks are characterized by solid balance sheets and steady cash flows. Most blue-chip stocks have a history of earning increasing dividends for their shareholders. These types of stocks are ideal for long-term investors who want to hold stocks for long periods.

- **Primary Market**

In a primary market, companies sell their shares directly to investors. In most cases, companies in primary markets sell to corporations and institutions rather than to individual investors. Hedge funds, mutual funds, and similar investors are typically the kind of investors that buy shares directly from companies in primary markets.

- **Secondary Markets**

In a secondary market, investors buy and sell shares amongst themselves. Individual investors buy shares in secondary markets. In this type of market, you can choose to buy shares of a particular company or a mix of different companies' shares in exchange-traded funds or EFTs.

- **Over-the-Counter Markets**

OTC markets are where companies that are not listed in exchanges like NYSE trade their shares. In OTC markets there is no public price for the shares and the value of the transaction is dependent on the buyer and seller.

- **Bid**

A bid is a price at which you want to buy the share.

- **Ask**

The ask is the price at which the seller wants to sell the share at

- **Spread**

The spread is the difference between the bids and sell prices of a stock. If you want to buy a stock at $50 and the buyer wants to sell it at $45, the spread, in this case, is $5.

- **Volatility**

Volatility refers to the movement of share prices in the market. When the price fluctuates widely within short periods of time then it is said to be highly volatile. The higher the volatility of a particular share, the higher the risk associated with it and also the higher the profit potential.

- **Dividend**

A dividend is the percentage of a company's earnings that is paid out to shareholders. Dividends can be paid out annually or quarterly depending on the company. Not all companies pay dividends to the shareholders.

- **Broker**

A broker is a trader who buys and sells shares for an investor for a fee or commission.

- **Bear Market**

A bear market refers to a downward trend in the market where stock prices are falling

- **Bull Market**

A bull market refers to an upward trend in the market where stock prices are rising.

- **Beta**

Beta is the measurement of the price of a stock relative to the movement of the whole market. If a stock moves 1.5 points for every 1-point move in the market, then it has a beta of 1.5.

- **Index**

An index is a measure that is used as a benchmark to gauge market performance. Some of the most famous indices include the Dow Jones and the S&P 500.

Chapter 2. Steps to Evaluate Your Financial Health, Setting, Goals (What to Consider Before Opening a New Account)

There are many ways to go about investing and knowing which path to take can be a daunting process. You can narrow down the possibilities to a strategy that works for you by evaluating your current financial situation. This should be done before you enter into your first trade. To be successful, an investor needs a clear picture of where they are going. Keep in mind this is not a one-time event. You should reevaluate your financial situation on an annual basis since it's going to be changing. When you find yourself in a different financial situation, your investment strategies will change over time.

Where

Establishing a starting point is the first step. You don't have to be a financial wizard, but you need to be aware of your present situation before jumping in and buying stocks. Consider the following scenario. An investor with a large personal debt that has an interest rate of 17% keeps putting money in the stock market, hoping to build wealth over time. That sounds reasonable, but most market returns are, going to be in the range of 5-10%. That means that someone in this situation is actually losing money.

Seek Liquidity

We are going to recommend that you look for assets you can sell.

The money can be used to pay debts, back taxes, or to seed investment capital. You'll want to list all of your assets by liquidity, which means how easily they can be converted into cash. You'll also want to consider how much cash you can raise by selling each item if you were to sell it. A house might have a lot more value than a television set, but you might sell the television set in 24 hours while you'd have to wait months to sell the house.

Dealing with Debts

Taking care of debts is one of the first things that a budding investor needs to do. While you might be anxious to get started with a large-scale investment plan if you have debts to take care of you might want to put it off. So, the first step in preparing your investment plan is to create a simple balance sheet. You don't have to be an accountant, and you're only doing this for yourself, but it needs to be honest and accurate.

You're going to want to put together a listing of all of your assets and liabilities. When compiling assets, include everything of value that you could possibly sell. This could be a computer that you're not using, a dusty TV in a room nobody goes into very often, or an old guitar. Selling things, you don't need can help you pay off debts faster and raise investment capital. You might object that you wouldn't raise much money but imagine having an extra $500 to $1,000 to start off with.

When listing your liabilities, you're going to want to know how much debt you have, what the interest rates are, and what your monthly payments are.

Monthly payments are less important than interest rates. Once you've listed all of your debts, you'll want to develop a plan to pay them off in a reasonable amount of time. There are many calculators available online, and you can also read many books on how to pay off debt. The series of books by debt guru Dave Ramsey is highly recommended. Here is an example of a good debt calculator:

https://www.creditkarma.com/calculators/debt_repayment/

You can use this calculator to figure out how long it will take to pay off a debt for a given monthly payment. You can enter the interest rate, and the time frame you would like along with the monthly payment you're willing to make. Start off with the current minimum payment in order to determine the time required to pay off the debt and work up from there.

In this example, we considered a $21,000 debt with a high 11% interest rate. Paying $450 a month would take five years to pay off the debt.

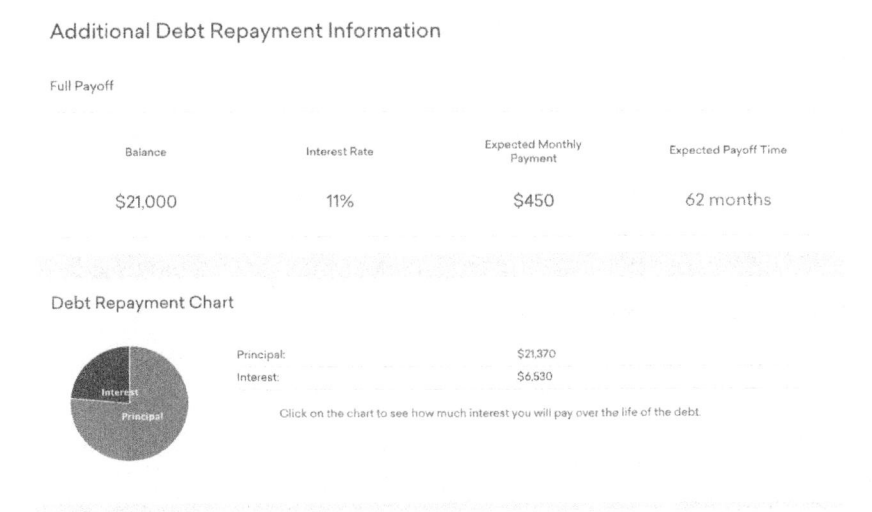

Additional Debt Repayment Information

Full Payoff

Balance	Interest Rate	Expected Monthly Payment	Expected Payoff Time
$21,000	11%	$450	62 months

Debt Repayment Chart

Principal: $21,370
Interest: $6,530

Click on the chart to see how much interest you will pay over the life of the debt.

That isn't a good situation to be in — do you want to saddle yourself with a $21,000 debt for five years?

When you have listed all of your debts, then you can prioritize them. In order to make the most progress in the shortest amount of time, it can be helpful to tackle the smallest debts first. This not only helps you get rid of your debt faster, but it will also have psychological benefits as you improve your financial situation.

If you have back taxes, you should make these a priority. The reason is that the government tacks on lots of fees and penalties, and if the tax debt is allowed to sit around, it can grow substantially in size. Get payment plans arranged to take care of these debts before they become unmanageable.

Take a look at your spending habits. Having material goods now isn't important if you plan to become a successful investor. You will be able to buy that BMW or Mercedes you want later when you can really afford it. For now, your focus should be on being able to direct your financial resources into your investments so that you can grow your wealth over time. Expensive toys, like a new car, can be a large financial drain. If you have car loans, consider getting out of the car and into a used car that is reliable but costs a lot less. From this point forward, don't use debt to finance purchases. Keep a credit card on hand for emergencies, but don't use it to buy things like books or groceries that should be paid for using cash. If you can't pay for something with cash, it can wait.

Having an Emergency Fund

Life is never fair, and we are all going to encounter emergencies.

Recent studies have shown that most Americans don't have enough cash on hand to pay a $500 bill. If you are in that situation, you need to rectify it before you jump in with a large-scale investment plan. Remember that paying off debt first is always the priority. Debt is a sink that sucks important financial resources down the drain that could be used for other purposes. However, it's important to start putting money away for an emergency fund to be prepared for the unexpected — and being able to pay for it without having to take on more debt. Or worse, getting into a situation where you can't get credit but still need to find money to pay emergency bills. Set aside a small amount of money that you can start depositing into a savings account that you won't touch unless there is an emergency. Over time, the goal should be to have enough cash on hand to take care of emergency bills ranging up to $5,000 and to have funds on hand to cover times when you might be unemployed.

Consider Additional Sources of Income

If you have a large amount of debt or find yourself in a situation where coming up with a significant amount of money to invest is difficult, you should consider taking action to increase your income. There are many paths to consider. You can start by looking for a higher-paying job.

Alternatively, you can look into taking a second job, at least until you are in a better financial situation. Another approach that can be used is to either take on "gigs" or short-term contract work.

This can be done online or by doing some side work with companies like Uber. You can even look into starting your own online business to generate more income.

This doesn't have to be a permanent situation, but you are going to want to get to a place where you are debt-free and can put $1,000 or more into the stock market every month.

Net Worth and Changes Over Time

When you've gathered everything together, you'll want to determine your net worth. You are doing this for yourself, so don't be embarrassed if it's in a bad position right now. Simply add up the total current value of your assets and liabilities and subtract the total value of the liabilities from the total value of your assets. This is your net worth. If you can compare the value of each asset now to the value it had at the beginning of the year; you can also calculate the change in your net worth in percentage terms.

Are You Ready to Invest?

If you are debt-free or have a plan in place to take care of your debts and to build an emergency fund, you are ready to begin investing. The first rule of investing is to never invest more than you can afford to lose. If you go about your investment plan carefully, the chances of losing everything are slim to none. That said it's a wise approach to invest as if that could really happen. So, you shouldn't be investing next month's house payment or your kid's college funds in the hopes of gaining returns. After you have taken care of your debts and emergency fund, add up all of your basic living expenses, so you know how much you actually need per month. Anything left over above that is the amount of money you can invest for now.

Determining Your Financial Goals

Once you are in a position to invest something — even if you can only put in $100 a month now because you're paying off large debts — it's time to sit down and figure out your financial goals. There are several things to keep in mind:

Age: Generally speaking, the older you are, the more conservative you should be in your investment approach. The reason for this is simple. When things go badly, it takes time to recover and get back on the road to profitability. The older you are, the less time you have to grow your wealth in the future. That means a market crash, or a bad investment has larger consequences than it would have if you had thirty years to recover. Financial advisors generally recommend that older investors put their money in safer investments, which means putting some money into bonds and safe investments like US Treasuries that preserve capital. In the stock market, the older investor will seek out more stable companies that are larger, and while they may be growing, they have slow and steady growth with lower levels of risk. Of course, age can cut both ways. Many people reach their fifties with little to no savings or investment. If that describes your situation, you're going to want to invest more aggressively to seek rapid growth. Younger people also want to invest more aggressively, as they have a time horizon that permits taking on more risk. But time horizon isn't the only factor if you have no capital to protect; you definitely want to be more aggressive.

Chapter 3. Risks in Investing in Stocks

Understanding risk and volatility are two of the most important things to keep in mind with the stock market.

There are many different types of risk in the stock market. Some are direct, such as a small company that has the *potential* to make gains because of innovative products. Others are indirect and external. You can't manage all types of risks. Some come out of the blue, like the 9/11 terrorist attacks or the 2008 financial crash. So, if you think that you can control every form of risk, take a deep breath and realize you can't. In this chapter, we are going to try and describe every major category of risk investor's face, and if possible, we'll suggest ways to deal with them.

Emotional and Person Risk

First and foremost, you can control the risks to your investments that come from personal factors. These include fear, impatience, and greed. Emotions like these can be hard to control, but learning to take charge of them is essential if you are going to be a successful investor.

When real money is on the line, these emotions can become strong and overpowering. You must not let that happen.

The most common problem when it comes to emotions and personal risk is fear. When a stock market starts looking bearish, many investors immediately jump ship. They are making a huge mistake. A good investor is not getting in and out of the market at the slightest sign of a problem. In fact, selling off when everyone else is could be one of the biggest mistakes individual investors make. By the way, that doesn't exempt large investors. Many professional traders are subject to the same emotions and exhibit the same behavior during downturns. Massive selloffs are what cause bear markets to develop.

First of all, remember that you are looking to hold your investments over the long term. So, the ups and downs of the market and even recessions are not a reason to sell them. Over the past 50 years, by far the worst stock market contraction happened in the 2008 financial crisis. However, even that was short-lived. People that sold off their investments were either faced with being out of the markets altogether or having to get back in the markets when prices were appreciating. The lifetimes of other major bear markets were similar or even more short-lived. The first lesson in managing personal risk is to hold your investments through downturns.

The second lesson is that rather than giving into fear, you should start to see market downturns as opportunities. When prices are rapidly dropping due to a market sell-off, you should be buying shares. It's impossible to know where the bottom of a market is, and you shouldn't concern yourself with that.

At any time that share prices are declining, it's an opportunity, and so you should be making regular stock purchases. In one year, two years, or five years down the road, on average, the stocks that you purchased in a downturn are going to be worth quite a bit more.

The second problem that arises as a part of personal risk is greed. Many people start seeing dollar signs when they begin investing. Having a get-rich-quick mentality is not compatible with successful investing. Your approach should be centered on slowly and steadily accumulating wealth and not making a quick buck. As you invest, you're going to be coming across claims that certain trades or stocks are the next best thing, but you're better off ignoring such claims. More often than not, they turn out to be false. The stock market is not a gambling casino, even though many people treat it that way. You can avoid succumbing to greed by maintaining a regular investment program and not being taken in by the temptation that you can profit from short-term swings or "penny stocks" that are going to supposedly take off.

Finally, there is the related problem of impatience. After the Great Depression, people developed a more reasonable and cautious approach to the stock market. They realized that you're not going to get rich in six months or a year. The idea of long-term investing became dominant.

Unfortunately, in recent years, this lesson seems to be getting lost. More people are behaving like traders rather than as investors. Far too many investors are being taken in by the seduction of being able to beat market returns. Instead of being impatient, you should realize that you're in it for the long haul. Rather than trying to make a few extra bucks now, you're seeking to build wealth.

Risk of Loss of Capital

Obviously, financial risk is something you face when investing. Theoretically, there is a chance that you will lose all the money you invest in the stock market. This can happen if you tie your fate to a small number of companies. Several well-known companies like Lumber Liquidators, Bear-Stearns, and GM have either had major problems or gone completely under. Investors may have lost large sums in the process. The way to deal with this is to avoid investing in a small number of companies. Later in the chapter, we will investigate diversification as an investment strategy.

You'll also want to pay attention to the types of companies you invest in. Putting all of your money into small-cap stocks, for example, is probably a bad idea. So is putting all of your money into emerging markets, or into one sector of the stock market. Again, the key message is diversification. It's the way to protect you from financial risk.

Market and Economic Risk

Some factors are beyond your control, and the economy inevitably cycles through slowdowns and downturns. The market will cycle along with the economy, and also experience crashes when the economy may be doing fine overall. This happened in 1987, for example.

While these factors are not under your control, how you react to them is under your control. As we discussed in the section on emotional risk, you should not panic when there is a downturn. Remain level-headed, and use downturns as a buying opportunity. They are always followed by a brighter day; your job is to have the patience to wait for it to arrive.

Interest Rate Risk

Changing interest rates can impact the markets. Although this is a book about stock market investing, you should have some awareness of how bond markets work. You should also be aware that investor money can flow back and forth between bond and stock markets depending on conditions.

One thing that bond markets offer is the safety of capital, especially when we are talking about U.S. government bonds. When interest rates are high, U.S. government bonds (and other types of bonds, including corporate and municipal bonds) become very attractive.

Interest rate changes have risks for bond investors, however. Bonds are traded on secondary markets. When interest rates rise, bond prices fall because older bonds that offer lower interest rates become less attractive. Conversely, when interest rates fall, older bonds that pay higher interest rates have more value than new bonds being issued that pay relatively low rates.

This doesn't directly affect a stock market investor, but if demand for bonds rises, that can mean less capital flowing into the stock market. Less demand means lower prices, so the market may see declines.

Also, as we'll see, you can invest in bonds through the stock market using exchange-traded funds. If you are using this method, you'll want to keep close tabs on interest rates. That means paying closer attention to the Federal Reserve and its quarterly announcements. You should be doing so even if you are not going to invest in bonds in any way.

Announcements on interest rate changes can have a large impact on stock prices. But as always, keep your eye on the long ball. If the markets react negatively to an increase in interest rates that can be an opportunity to buy undervalued stocks.

Political Risk and Government

Government and politics can create big risks in the stock market. International events can cause market crashes, and these days even a tweet from the President can cause markets to rise and fall. Lately, some politicians have also been discussing breaking up the big tech companies. Others are talking about investigating them. Such talk — and worse actions— can have a negative impact on the markets. Part of your job as an investor is to keep a close eye on the news. You're going to want to know what's happening so that you can adjust if necessary.

Inflation Risk

Inflation hasn't been high in decades. However, in the late 1970s inflation rates were routinely in the double digits. Hopefully, that isn't going to be something that happens anytime soon, because high inflation rates can eat your returns alive. If the stock market is appreciating at 7% per year, but inflation is 14%, you can see that it's like having debt but investing in stocks — it's a losing proposition. Right now, inflation risk is very low, but you'll want to have some awareness of it and always keep tabs on it. High inflation rates also tend to go hand-in-hand with high interest rates, since the Federal Reserve will raise rates to try and slow down inflation. That means that bonds might become more attractive when inflation gets out of control.

Taxes and Commissions

Finally, we have the risk imposed by taxes. Of course, we are all going to be hit with taxes no matter where our money comes from. However, you need to take into account the taxes that you are going to pay when it comes to any gains you realize on the stock market. Part of being a successful investor is having an understanding of how much your taxes are cutting into your profits. If you are investing for the long-term, it will be less of an issue. But keep in mind that taxes can really eat into short-term trades. Frequent, short-term traders also face risk from commissions and fees. If you execute a lot of trades, the commissions can add up. This is not an issue for long-term investors.

Risk vs. Return

One of the fundamental trade-offs that an investor will make is risk vs. return. Generally speaking, the higher the risk, the greater the *possibility* of good returns. In 1998, Amazon was a pretty high-risk investment. While it had potential, major bookstores like Borders and Barnes & Noble dominated the space. Amazon was on shaky ground at the time, and another company could have come in and competed successfully for online book sales. That never happened, and Amazon ended up dominating book sales and expanding widely across retail and into cloud computing. That risk has translated into massive returns. A $10,000 investment in 1998 would be worth more than $1 million today.

But hindsight is 20/20. Today, there are similar opportunities all around us, but it's hard to know which ones will end up being successful over the long term. If you are an aggressive investor, part of your job will be estimating which companies are the best bets for the future.

Chapter 4. How to Invest in Stocks (How to Buy Your First Stock)

How to Get Start

Stock may seem incredibly intimidating for those starting in the investment world. It looks like a completely different world, and the hardest step for most is the beginning. However, it is quite simple to get started in stock investments. First, one must set goals for themselves and determine how they would like to invest in a stock. By writing down goals and ensuring that the investor's money is used in the best possible way, the investor is helping them yield the highest return on their investment. Once the individual's goals are made clear, they must plan on how to meet those goals. After this, they may choose the best investment method for achieving these goals. Then, it must be decided on where exactly the investor will go to invest their money. It is crucial, as this will be the platform by which the investor will trade their stocks. After this, the investor must open an account with whomever they choose. Before they start trading, the investor must make an initial investment using this account. While doing so, they may have to link their bank account to their stock trading account. The investor must then begin the process of buying and selling stocks using this account. Although this seems like a lengthy process, it is quite simple.

Planning and Meeting Goals

Investors must familiarize themselves with their goals. It is quite helpful to write down one's goals in each area and put them somewhere that is easily accessible. It is useful to have measurable goals to reach. This way, there may be a specific period and amount that may be assigned to the targets. It may help to come up with monthly goals. For instance, the investor may start with the purchase of 100 shares of stock in February. They may wish to increase that to 150 shares by March, 200 shares by April, and so on. This way, the investor may have a period to achieve their goals. It will allow them to measure their progress easily.

To set proper goals, one must reflect upon their past. How much will the investor be able to set aside for stock realistically? If one's goals are not realistic, it may become discouraging and set the investor back from their full potential. The investor must consider any past investments they have made. They must consider what worked and what did not. It is crucial to consider income and expenses when investing, and one must also consider any savings goals that one has. This will make it more apparent what may be invested in stocks.

Without a clear guide on how to invest, the investor will lack direction. It may lead to spur-of-the-moment decisions, and the investor may regret these choices. There may be some periods where one will not trade, as it won't be as profitable. Perhaps the market is down, and the trader does not wish to sell any stock. Perhaps the market is up, and the trader does not want to buy any stock. There will be events such as vacations, holidays, stressful events, or emergencies.

One must also consider how much money they have. Although it is possible to double one's money in a year, it is not likely for a beginner to do so. One may also choose to invest one time and hold it, or they may choose to invest more into their account often. This time and amount will depend on the investor and their financial situation.

The investor must also choose a strategy. They may wish to buy and sell stocks or to buy and hold stocks. They may even consider options trading. Whichever method that the investor chooses, there will be different goals to fit those strategies.

Long-term goals may be set to help the investor. Although planning for the following year may help the investor, longer periods may prove even more beneficial. Perhaps the investor wishes to acquire a million dollars worth of stock in the succeeding ten years. Perhaps the investor wishes to save a certain amount for retirement, which they wish to have by the next 25 years. Whatever the end goal is, the investor must make that clear so that they can begin working towards it immediately. Once a proper plan is created for meeting the investor's goals, they may move to the next step.

Choosing an Investment Method

After the investor has set goals and created a plan to meet them, it is time to decide on which investment method they wish to pursue. For those that wish to trade on their own completely, the DIY (do-it-yourself) method is the best fit. The investor may conduct all their trades online, making transfers from the bank manually or automatically. It will allow full control of one's investments. There will also be complete independence over what the investor wishes to buy and sell, how much they wish to trade, and how often they wish to trade.

They will, however, need to dedicate time to researching, making any transfers, trading, and other procedures. There is also a higher risk for this choice, as a beginning investor will not have the education that a financial advisor will. They also won't be under the control of a Robo-Advisor. However, all the profit that is made by the investor will be theirs to keep. They won't have to pay commission and fees outside of any required by the broker that they use.

The least independent approach to investing in stock is by hiring a financial advisor. It is for those who do not wish to touch their stock at all and to have it fully regulated for them. Hesitant beginners may benefit from this method. It is important to remember, however, that this method tends to be the costliest. It is most beneficial for those with higher assets and larger portfolios. It is also important to choose an investor that will work to meet the investor's goals, not just the goals of themselves. Therefore, the investor must set specific goals for themselves and how they wish to invest their money. They may more easily communicate with the advisor their desires, which may be carried out for them.

Choosing a Stockbroker

When investing for oneself, a proper stockbroker must be chosen. This will depend on the individual's needs and wants. For some, their bank that they already operate offers stock investments through their bank. This is a quick and simple option, as their money will already be linked through the bank, and they may already be familiar with their style. There may also be options for financial advisors in the bank that are free of charge. Otherwise, the investor must research their options before settling on a broker.

When choosing a stockbroker, the investor should research any fees (transaction fees, maintenance fees, etc.), minimum funds required to open an account, any commission collected by the stockbroker, and accessibility. The investor may prefer a specific type of formatting for their broker to have. There may also be free education, customer service, and other ways to make investing easier for the investor.

The investor must choose the option that will allow them to make the highest return on their investments. The investor should keep in mind which services they are likely to use most frequently, and they should choose the broker that charges the least to use those services. There may be transactional fees, which are costs for buying and selling stocks. Many beginning investors tend to forget this, so it is essential to take this into account.

Opening an Account

When opening an account, there are often a few steps that are required. This is typically not a lengthy process, but the investor should be aware of the potential actions associated with opening an account.

The first step when opening an online account is typically to create an account. This will consist of a username and password, as well as some personal information. This may include setting goals, determining which types of features the investor wishes to use, and the investor's experience level. This information will help to create the optimal experience for the investor.

There may also be an application for the account to ensure that the investor is qualified to hold the account. There may also be an agreement stating that the investor assumes all the risks of investing and understands that the money is not insured or guaranteed. Initial Investment and Linking Accounts

During the application process, the investor will most likely be prompted to fund the account. This can be done in several ways. The investor may transfer the funds electronically via an EFT (Electronic funds transfer). This is transferring the money from a linked bank account and will most likely only take one business day to transfer. The investor may also choose to make a wire transfer, which is a transfer directly from the bank. It is important to consider how much to invest in the account initially carefully. For those just starting, there may not be much money to invest at first. The minimum investment amounts for the broker should be looked over beforehand.

Chapter 5. When to Buy and Sell Stock

When to Sell a Stock

Determining when to sell a stock is a decision that even the world's best investors wrestle with. Warren Buffett has said that his holding period for a stock is forever. Does Buffett really hold every stock that he buys forever? Of course not! The point that he is making is that you should always purchase a stock with the intention of holding it forever; therefore, make sure your money has been put into your best investment ideas. An investor should leave his or her portfolio intact for at least five years, as long as the fundamentals for which a particular stock was purchased do not deteriorate. Investors should pay no attention to a stock's price volatility because it is a normal part of the investment cycle. As a long-term investor, there will be times when it makes sense to sell or reduce your position in stock earlier than you had planned. Next, we will talk about different circumstances in which you should consider selling a stock or reducing your position in a stock.

- **The Time Frame** — If you need the money within five years, it should not be invested in stocks. It would be best to invest your money in safe and stable short-term instruments. Money market accounts, money market funds, and short-term certificates of deposits would be better options. Since the Great Recession struck, some investment professionals now recommend that you not invest any money in stocks that will be needed within 10 years.
- **An Overvalued Stock** — When a stock is significantly overvalued, sell it. Take the proceeds from the sale and invest them into other

undervalued stocks that you have researched. The P/E ratio is still one of the best indicators of value. For example, if a stock has traded at an average P/E of 15 for the last seven to 10 years and the business is thriving, but the stock currently trades at a P/E of 30 or more on consistent or increasing EPS, you should seriously consider selling the stock. The PEG ratio is also a very effective method for determining if a stock is now overvalued.

- **Too Much Debt** — Too much debt is dangerous for any business because there's always the chance that a business may be unable to pay its debt. Too much debt also puts a business at greater risk of failure if a downturn in the industry or economy were to occur. Upon entering the 2007 recession, thousands of businesses here in the United States literally disappeared overnight and that was before things really got bad.
- **Too Much Risk** — You have already learned the importance of staying away from investments that are too risky. Sometimes new management will come to a business and begin to implement new policies; along with that implementation, they will knowingly or unknowingly expose a business to greater risk. If you purchased the stock of a business that stayed away from very risky practices, but the business has now begun to display risky behaviors that make you uncomfortable, sell the stock and find yourself a better investment.
- **Loss of Competitive Advantage** — You have also learned that we should only be purchasing the stocks of businesses that have a durable competitive advantage. When a business changes its business

model, resulting in it losing its competitive advantage, sell the stock.
- **The Portfolio Lacks Balance or Diversification** — It's very easy for your best performing stock to become the largest holding in your portfolio, and there's absolutely nothing wrong with that. The problem arises when the stock makes up more than 20-25% of your portfolio's total value. Legendary investor, Jim Slater suggests that individual investors limit the number of funds invested in a single stock within their portfolios to a maximum of 15%. When your portfolio becomes heavily weighted in one stock, consider reducing your position of that stock to bring more balance and better diversification into your portfolio.
- **Stock Reaches Its Fair Value** — Our goal as investors should always be to purchase a stock at a discount to its fair value and it is recommended at least a 25% discount to its fair value. By doing so, when you sell a stock that has reached its fair value, you are guaranteed a gain of at least 25% from the sale. This is a disciplined approach to selling a stock. According to research, it was common for Benjamin Graham to sell a stock once it had a 50% gain in price. If the future prospects of a particular stock look good, you may decide to sell only a portion of the stock, such as half of its shares, and hold on to the rest when using this approach.
- **When Your Analysis is Found to Be Flawed**— There will be times when an investor will be very detailed and careful in his or her analysis of a particular company or its stock, only to find out later that his or her analysis is incorrect or flawed.

Whether a stock should be sold at that time depends on the seriousness of the error and its impact on the long-term performance of the business. So, when you find that you have incorrectly analyzed a particular business, it is essential for you to take a serious look at all available information to determine whether or not to sell the stock or to continue holding it. One thing is certain, as an investor, you will not always be right when analyzing a company or its stock.

There is no clear-cut way to determine the optimal time to sell a stock. There will be times that you will sell a stock because it has not performed well, only to see it skyrocket and double or triple in price soon after you sell it. There will also be occasions when you have purchased what seems to be the perfect stock, only to watch it tumble in price and for no apparent reason. Learn what you can from these events and move on. Even Peter Lynch, Jim Slater, and other great investors have sold stocks too early or too late. It's going to happen sometimes.

When to Buy a Stock

After the investor funds their account, it is time to start trading the stocks. It must be decided what stock, how much of the stock, and how the investor wishes to buy. Once these factors are decided, the investor must buy the stock. It is usually as simple as searching the stock symbol and selecting "buy." It is best to wait until the stock is at a low, but the investor must also begin investing as early as possible in experiencing the benefits of investing. When the stock is bought, it will typically take a bit to process and for the broker to receive these funds. After that, it will show up in the online portfolio of the investor. When it is time to sell this stock, the investor may typically visit their portfolio and click "sell" on the desired stock.

Starting out as a stock investor is quite simple. The investor must follow a few steps to become a stock trader. They must choose an investment method, select a stockbroker, open an account, a fund that account, and they will be ready to go.

Your very first stock trade can be frightening - not to mention confounding. You've done your stock research, you believe you've found a winner, and now you're all set to put your brand-new brokerage account to excellent usage and begin trading — nevertheless, you're not quite sure how to "carry it out."

Trade "execution" is just an elegant technique for describing an exchange. To "trade" typically describes a particular kind of investing method, so certifying your use of the term "trade" with "carry out" lets other financiers understand that you're going over a particular exchange.

The real-time it takes to perform your trade can move from broker to broker and market to market. (The SEC requires that all brokerage companies supply documents quarterly to the basic population about the handling of their customer orders).

Your broker will unquestionably put your order through their complicated trading computer system network to get a hold of your shares when you do put in your order. In many cases, your order will never ever leave the broker —

your brokerage company ought to clean out shares of the organization you're purchasing from its stock.

You have a couple of choices when it comes to trading stocks beyond merely selling and purchasing. Basically, you get shares of a particular stock and sell them, relying on that the stock will diminish in worth, leaving the distinction between the selling rate and ultimate repurchase rate in your pocket.

Stock Order Types

Naturally, buying stocks is similarly more complex than only one purchase. There are numerous different approaches for considering your purchase, all going concerning cost, the time point of confinement, which is simply the start.

Anyhow, what are your alternatives for purchasing stock? There are 5 various types of stock orders that your broker will likely let you utilize.

A market order is a demand to sell a stock or buy at the existing market value. Market orders are quite a great deal for the basic stock order, and because the capability is typically performed instantly.

Something to keep as a primary top priority with a market order is the way you do not manage the amount you pay for your stock purchase or sale; the marketplace does.

The speed with which online market orders have actually launched might have made this less of a danger than it used to be. The market still moves quicker.

Some individuals do not have problems with this, for those that do this, imperfection can be met with a breaking point order.

- **Point of Confinement Order**

    A breaking point order can keep you from purchasing or selling your stock at a rate that you do not want, possibly assisting you in keeping a strategic range from a horrible choice. On the off possibility that the cost is a misdirected base and not in tune with the market, nevertheless, the order will never ever be made.

    Keep in mind that some brokers charge more for point of confinement orders, as the trade might not go through.

- **Stop-loss Order**

    Stop-loss orders, when that price is reached, transform into market orders. The target price is hit, and the trade is executed at market value.

- **Stop-Limit Order**

    Stop-limit orders are also stopped orders based on hanging tight at a particular expense. Stop-limit orders end up being point of confinement orders when the target cost is reached as opposed to market orders.

    Changing into a breaking point order can be something useful for a stop order, staying away from particular threats. On the occasion that the shares topple to $20.00 at the very same time, then instantly shoot back up, your market order might go through in any case.

- **Tracking Stop**

Generally, this is a stop order based upon a portion modification in the market cost instead of setting a target cost.

You can pick to what degree the order stays open when you put an order into your broker. Naturally, orders are day orders, indicating that they are signed up until completion of the trading day. Outstanding till-canceled orders stay open until you really enter and cancel them.

Chapter 6. How to Generate Passive Income from the Stock Market

Income investing is a little bit of a different ballgame than growth investing. In this case, we are seeking out companies that pay dividends. That means ignoring a lot of high growth stocks like Amazon and Netflix. It also means ignoring disruptive companies with potential like Tesla. When you are an income investor, you are looking to make a certain level of income from your stock holdings. That may be now, or it may be in the future. But your portfolio is going to look quite different from a growth investor, and even a value-oriented growth investor.

Yield

Start compiling a diverse list of companies that pay dividends that you find interesting. In each case, track the yield, which is the dividend divided by the share price. That will help you compare apples-to-apples when judging one dividend stock against another. Keep in mind that you are going to be seeking some kind of balance, so buying up stocks with the highest yields isn't the best philosophy. To see why to consider a company called consolidated communications. They pay a yield of 32%. The problem is, it's a penny stock. That means it's only $4 or so a share. Most analysts are rating it a SELL. A glance at the chart indicates it has dropped from a $29 share price over the past couple of years, and yet it's still rated as being overvalued. These are major red flags.

Dividend

You may also be interested in the actual dividend payment, and not just the yield. IBM pays $6 a share, but Apple only pays $1.55 a share. So, you'd have to own more than three Apple shares for every share of IBM you could buy in order to get the same annual income from your stocks. Since IBM is cheaper on a per-share basis, that is something to take into consideration.

Dividend Growth

For any stock that you invest in, you're going to want to look at the history of their dividend payments. The ideal dividend stock is one that pays higher dividends over time. IBM is a great example because they paid consistent dividends through the 2008 financial crisis, and they have been increasing their dividends since then. Dividend growth ensures that your dividend payments will keep up with or exceed inflation.

DRIPS and Reinvesting

If you have a large amount of capital available right now, you can buy up shares of stock and start living off the dividend payments. However, if you are looking at a long-term investment program, you are going to want to reinvest your dividends. In the future, you're going to want to have as many shares as possible, so taking cash out now simply doesn't make sense. Instead, the payments from dividends should be used to purchase additional shares. Some companies even allow you to purchase fractional shares with the money.

A DRIP is a Dividend Reinvestment Program. In this case, the company will automatically take any dividends you earn and use them to buy additional shares. This will help enforce discipline in case you get tempted to cash out your dividends and waste the money on a trip or new car. Instead, the company will force you to save for the future.

Exchange-Traded Funds

The possibility of using exchange-traded funds to meet your investment goals always exists. In this case, you can seek out an ETF that invests in dividend stocks. You will still receive dividend payments, and the fund will have built-in diversification. When looking at ETFs to use for dividend investing, be sure to focus on yield, and pick funds that have the highest yields. Many investors can do a mixture of both; you could invest in ETFs while also investing in specific companies like IBM.

Alternative Investments

The world of dividend investing isn't restricted to traditional stock investing. You can also invest in the following:

- REITS
- MLPs
- BDCs

A REIT is a real estate trust. This is a company that owns hard property assets and rents them out. The types of property are quite varied. For example, you can invest in REITs that own rental homes, apartments, or commercial real estate. There are also REITs that own hotels and resorts. In fact, any type of property that you can think of is represented by at least one REIT. But interestingly, there are REITs that have great prospects for the future because they are technology-related. For example, some REITs own cell phone towers, and there are others that own cloud computing.

REITs pay high dividends, and they trade like stocks on the stock market. Investing in REITs is a good way to get some exposure to real estate and other types of property ownership.

An MLP is a master limited partnership. These companies are midstream energy companies that transport oil and gas, own pipelines, or own refinement facilities. These are great investments to consider, and they also pay high dividends. You also invest in them by purchasing shares on the stock market. These types of investments are particularly noteworthy because the companies are partnerships and not corporations. When you invest, you become a limited partner. This means that you can deduct company expenses on your tax returns. Essentially, a large share of the income from an MLP is tax-free.

The final alternative investment that we are looking at is called a BDC, or Business Development Corporation. They also trade on stock exchanges and pay dividends. These are financial companies that invest in small to mid-sized companies that need cash. They can provide loans to companies or take an ownership stake.

When to Cash Out

Cashing out is a personal decision. By cashing out, in this case, we don't mean selling off your shares. What we mean is when should you stop reinvesting and start taking dividends as cash income. The answer is you start doing this when the level of dividend payments you receive starts matching your desired income.

Don't be afraid to shake up your portfolio. If you find an investment that suits your needs better than stocks you are currently invested in, then you should be ready to sell some of your shares and invest in the other stock. There is no reason for you to be locked into a particular stock, you can buy shares in other companies and then start getting dividend payments from them in the next upcoming cycle.

Fundamentals Always Matter

No matter which path you choose, when dividend investing, you want to pay close attention to the fundamentals. In the end, fundamentals are what matters. A company with good fundamentals is going to be a good investment. So, you'll want some trade-off between solid fundamentals, yield, and dividend payment that suits your goals. Remember to always think long-term.

Bond Investing

Finally, if you are looking for an income investing portfolio, consider buying exchange-traded funds that invest in bonds.

As we discussed earlier, there is a wide array of choices, allowing you to find the right amount of risk and the right interest payments. You'll want to look at the yields of the bond funds. Some have high rates of growth and high yields. That is, you can achieve growth as well as income by investing in bond funds too. The advantage of using ETFs is that you can avoid the hassle of trying to invest in bond markets.

Chapter 7. The Main Mistakes of a Beginner

Mistakes happen in every field, sector, and industry. Some are always anticipated, while others happened unexpectedly. When it comes to stock trading, there are several mistakes that you can make. Understanding these mistakes can help you avoid them, thus ending up successful in your stock investments. Here are some of the common mistakes made by most investors, beginners, and professional traders alike:

Failure to Understand the Trade

It is always wrong to invest in a trade or business you know nothing about. It is a great mistake to engage in stock trading when you do not understand the business and financial models involved. You can avoid this mistake by taking the time to research the stock market and stock trading before investing your money. Know the different markets, the driving forces, as well as trading procedures.

Most investors tend to buy stocks from the latest companies and industries they know very little about. Although such companies may look promising, it is difficult to determine whether they will continue to exist. Understanding a specific company gives you a better hand over other investors. You will be able to make accurate predictions about the company or industry, which may bring you more profit. You will quickly tell when the business is booming, stagnating, or closing way before other investors get this information.

Individuals who do not take time to study companies miss out on future trends of these companies. Failing to establish such trends leads to several missed opportunities. For instance, a person who invests in a company that is higher than his capital may quickly lose all his investment. That is why it is always advisable that you invest in the industry you understand better. For instance, if you are a surgeon, you can invest in stocks that deal with medicine or related stocks. Lawyers can invest in companies that generate income through litigation, and so on.

Impatience

The stock market is for patient investors. It is a slow but steady form of investment. Although it bears various opportunities that can bring you money, you cannot make enough profit in one day. Most stock investors are always faced with the challenge of being patient. Some end up losing trade positions before they mature in the quest to make quick money. Exiting the market too early will always cost you some returns. As a new investor, you must never expect your investment portfolio to perform more than its capability, as this will always lead to a disaster. Remain realistic in terms of the time, duration, and resources needed to earn from the market.

Failure to Diversify

Another mistake that easily causes disaster is the failure to diversify. Professional investors do not have a problem with this since they can easily profit from a single type of stock. However, young investors must be able to diversify to secure their investment. Some of them do not stick to this principle. Most of these lose a great fortune as soon as they get onto the stock market. As you seek to invest, remember the rule of thumb governing stock diversity. This states that you should not invest more than 10% of your capital in one type of stock.

Getting Too Connected with a Certain Company

The essence of trading in stock is to make a profit. Sometimes, investors get too deep into a certain company that they forget that it is all about the shares and not the company itself. Being too attached to a company may cloud your judgment when it comes to stock trading since you may end up buying stocks from this company instead of getting the best deal on the market. As you learn more about companies, always remember that you are into the business to make money, besides creating relationships.

Investment Turnover

Investment turnover refers to the act of entering and exiting positions at will. This is one other mistake that destroys great investments. It is only beneficial to institutions that seek to benefit from low commission rates. Most stock trading positions charge transaction fees. The more frequently you buy and sell, the more you pay in terms of transaction fees. You, therefore, need to be careful when entering positions. Do not get in or exit too early. Have a rough idea of when you want to close positions so that you do not miss some of the long-term benefits of these positions.

Timing the Market

Market timing results in high investment turnover. It is not easy to successfully time the market. On average, only 94% of stock trading returns are acquired without the use of market timing. Most traders time the market as a way of attempting to recover their losses. They want to get even by making some profit to counter a loss. This is always known as a cognitive error in behavioral finance. Trying to get even on the stock market will always result in double losses.

Trading with Emotions

Allowing your emotions to rule is one of the things that kill your stock investment returns. Most people get into the market for fear of losses or thirst to make returns too fast. As a young trader, you must ensure that greed and fear do not overwhelm your decision-making. Stock prices may fluctuate a lot in the short-term; however, this may not be the case in the long term, especially for large-cap stocks. This means that you may get lower profits in the short term, but these may increase in the long term. Understanding this will help you avoid closing trades when it is not the right time yet.

Setting Unrealistic Expectations

This always occurs when dealing with small-cap stocks such as penny stocks. Most investors buy such stocks with the expectation that the prices will change drastically. Sometimes this works, but it is not a guarantee. To make great fortunes, people invest a lot of capital in these stocks, and then the prices do not change much. If these investors are not prepared for such an eventuality, they may feel frustrated and may quit the business completely. However, this is something that you must be able to manage if you want to grow your investment. Do not expect more than what a certain type of stock can deliver.

Using Borrowed Money

This is probably one of the greatest mistakes that investors make. Some investors get carried away with the returns they are making. As a way of getting more profits, they borrow money and use it to enter more stock positions. This is a very dangerous move and can result in a lot of stress. Stock trading is like gambling. You are not always sure how much you take home at the end of each trade. It is therefore not advisable for you to invest borrowed money in it.

As you try to avoid these mistakes, you must also avoid getting information from the wrong sources. Some traders have lost a fortune because they relied on the wrong sources for stock information. It is important to isolate a small number of people and places where you will seek guidance from. Do not be a person that follows the crowd. Take time before investing in new stock opportunities. Carry out proper due diligence, especially with small-cap stocks since these involve a lot of risks. Remember, you must trade carefully and implement expert advice if you want to succeed in stock trading.

Chapter 8. Insider Tricks Used by Professional Traders

An investor should always be on the lookout for signals that might be clues about their investments. One signal you should be keeping an eye on is the actions taken by the insiders with a company. Are they sticking by the company and investing in it? Or do they seem to be running away from it despite amazing stock prices? These can be important clues as to the health and intermediate future of the company. One thing you need to keep tabs on is whether or not the insiders are buying or selling shares of the company. You'll also want to note major departures from the company. Of course, the company is going to make up some pleasant story about why some major figure is leaving. You know, they want to spend more time with their grandmother. But is that really what's going on? If other news or more signals are indicating otherwise, including insider moves, you might view such news with a negative eye. People often leave a sinking ship.

Insider Trading

Here we aren't talking about criminal activity, but rather a company members themselves who own shares of the company that they are associated with. A good indication that people are confident in the future of their company is finding out that they own and are buying more shares of stock in their own company. On the other hand, if they are selling off their shares, that can be a sign that the people actually running the company or involved with it don't have that much confidence in its future.

It's actually possible to find out what company insiders are doing when it comes to shares of stock in their own company. The Securities and Exchange Commission requires them to file publicly available reports. You can find publicly filed reports on a government website known as "Edgar." It can be found here:

https://www.sec.gov/edgar.shtml

"Insiders" will file various forms, including an initial form that they have to submit to the government indicating their insider status with the company. This is called form 3.

If you are researching this data, you're going to want to pay special attention to form 4 and form 144. On form 4, any transactions involving a large number of shares are recorded. So, if the insider bought a large number of shares, it would be recorded on form 4. Also, if they sold a large number of shares, it's going to be reported on form 4.

If a single insider is selling shares, that doesn't necessarily mean anything. However, if you notice that multiple insiders are off-loading their shares, pay attention. That might be an indication that a large number of people who are in the know about the company's prospects aren't confident about the company's future.

Form 144 is related to a special class of stock called restricted stock. This is stock that the insider was provided as compensation for employment. If they decide to unload it after a required holding period, this will be noted with form 144.

In summary, if insiders are confident that the company is doing well and has solid long-term prospects, they are probably going to be buying shares in the company, not trying to get rid of them. You will want to take this kind of information and incorporate it into the larger picture of course. It's important to consider all the indicators for the company and not get lost in the details of focusing on one sign. So, if you notice that there is a large sell-off, you'll want to check other information like the company's latest earnings reports.

Quantity also Matters

Don't get alarmed if people sell a small number of shares. When they are trying to divest their own portfolio of any interest in the company, it is when you should take notice.

Congressional Insiders

A few years ago, the news program 60 Minutes did an interesting investigation. They found that members of Congress were playing the role of insiders at many companies and getting advantageous stock buys as a result. Unfortunately, there isn't much we can do about that, but it's good to have awareness about it.

Stock Buybacks

Stock buybacks can be a good sign or a bad sign. If a company is doing well, a stock buyback can be used as a way for a company to pass on profits to investors. However, stock buybacks can also be an indicator that a company is heading for trouble. The first thing to consider is that the company has lower than expected earnings. In that case, a company might use a stock buyback in order to artificially boost their indicators on the stock market. Buying back shares of stock, if done on a large enough scale, can alter important metrics like the price per earnings ratio and earnings per share. If you have fewer shares but the same earnings, earnings per share are going to look more favorable. They can do this in the hopes of artificially boosting the value of the stock and hence it's the market price. Consider an example. Suppose that a company has $500 in earnings and 100 shares. The earnings per share are $5. If they buy back 50 shares, then you still have $500 in earnings, but with 50 shares, so now the earnings per share are $10. That looks better to investors taking a cursory look at the stock, but in reality, the company's prospects haven't changed.

Another negative possibility is that the company has stagnated. If companies are out of ideas and not pursuing new ones, they aren't investing a large amount of money into research and development. That means they have cash sitting around and using a stock buyback could be a simple way to unload the cash.

You'll also want to check the price-to-earnings ratio and look up to see if the stock is overvalued. It can be a bad sign when a company is buying back overvalued shares.

Another question to ask is, where is the company getting the cash used for the buyback? Hopefully, they have enough money on hand to do it. But if they are borrowing money for the share buyback, that is definitely a sign that the company is unhealthy.

If you have invested in a company and they engage in a share buyback, you'll want to investigate further to find out what's behind it. In many cases, it's not something to worry about. However, sometimes it's an indicator that the future with this company is not so bright.

Stock Splits

Another corporate action you will need to be aware of is a stock split. Companies can do stock splits or reverse stock splits. In a stock split, a share is converted from 1 share to 2 or 3 or more shares. That immediately changes the price per share and impacts metrics like earnings per share. Imagine that a company has a share trading at $100, and it has 100 shares outstanding, and earnings per share of $5, meaning they have a price to earnings ratio of $20. If they do a 2-1 split, now there are 200 shares. The amount of money invested in the company hasn't changed, so the share price immediately drops to $50 a share. Now you have twice the number of shares in your portfolio, so the value of your investment hasn't changed. Earnings per share would be cut in half and would be reported as $2.50. The price-to-earnings ratio would remain at $20.

One reason a company might do a stock split is to reduce the price of a share, in order to attract more investors.

A stock trading at $1,000 a share might be unaffordable for a lot of small investors. If a company was interested in attracting more small investors, they might to a 4-1 stock split and drop the share price to $250 per share. A stock split for a high-priced stock can also increase liquidity. That is, it will increase the ease with which you can sell your shares. Very high-priced stocks will have large bid-ask spreads, which can make them harder to sell. Doing a split and bringing the price back down to a lower level can reduce the bid-ask spread and make it easier for investors to sell their shares.

A reverse stock split is going to reduce the number of shares that you own. So, if you own 100 shares and they did a 1-2 reverse split, you would only own 50 shares after that. If the share price had been $100, it would rise to $200 after the split. Remember that the amount of money invested remains the same before and after the split, so the share price also has to change if the number of shares changes.

Chapter 9. Tips and Tricks for Successful Stocks Trading

There are some tips and tricks that you can keep up your sleeve to help you invest in stocks. Let us look at some of them.

Always Be Informed

You need to be informed about what happens in the market. This is the only way you can trust your decisions. You should go through different resources and publications if you want to obtain more information about the various stocks in the market.

Buy Low, Sell High

This is a strategy that most investors will use. It is always good to buy low and sell high, and you must follow this to the tee. It is when you do this that you can expect to make large profits in the market. When you buy low and sell high, you will purchase a stock at its lowest value and sell it at its highest value. It will be easy for you to determine when the stock price will reach the highest rate based on some methods and data you collect. You need to ensure that you always act according to the data that you have collected. Experts recommend that it is a good idea to buy stocks the minute the market opens. Most stocks reach their highest price in the afternoon, and that is when you should sell them.

Scalping

This is a very popular technique in the stock market. When you use this technique, you can always buy and sell stocks within a matter of a few seconds. Your purchases and sales depend on how fast you are. This is a very strange method, but it is very effective, especially in volatile markets. Let us assume that you purchased a stock at 10:00 A.M. and sold it at 10:02 A.M. The price of that stock is $3, and the selling price is $5. So, in a matter of two minutes, you made a $2 profit per share, and this is a great profit for a scalper. This does not seem like a profit, but if you do this at least twenty or thirty times a day, you can make a huge profit. You should only use this form of trading once you have enough experience in the market. If you want to take up this technique, you should have at least a year's worth of experience to help you make the right decisions.

Short Selling

Many traders use the concept of short selling when they invest in the market. Short selling refers to when you need to borrow stock from the holder and sell it to another buyer. Then, you will wait for the stock price to fall before you give the stocks back to the lender. This is one of the easiest ways in which you can capitalize on the volatility of the prices. You must make the right decisions about the investments you make and not invest or borrow useless stocks. You must always ensure that you maintain a wide margin that will make a few mistakes. You should ensure that you have enough capital to support any other investments if things never work out. It is always good to buy shares back at the earliest if you believe that the price of the stocks will continue to increase.

Identify the Pattern

It is important to remember that stocks and every other stock in the market will follow a pattern. Once you notice this pattern and understand it, you can invest in stocks successfully. This pattern has all the information you need about the high and low points of the stocks and gathers some information on how you can trade between those points. It is important to have the history of the stock with you since it will help you determine the previous trend and predict the future trend of the stock.

Look at the Results

Every company is result-oriented, which means that the report published by the company will tell you how well the company is doing. The report that the company shares will shed some light on how well it is doing in the market. You should go through this report to ensure that you are making the right choice. The data collection results should show you that you could make enough profits when you invest in it. A small company will always aim to sell a large volume of stocks, and if you are impressed with the company and its numbers, you can invest in the stocks of that company. Remember that a company only publishes the results quarterly. Therefore, you need to look at all the results before you invest in the company.

Look at the Company Name

When choosing to invest in the stock market, you should understand that its name does matter. You must see if the company is well known and is doing well in the market. You can invest in a company that does not have any significant changes. Some people steer clear of such companies. If you are not a fundamentalist and are willing to take on a few risks, you can use technical analysis to help you make the decision. It is always good to learn more about the company if you choose to invest in shares in that company.

Understand the Company Better

You need to look at how the stock performs in the market, but it is important to spend some time understanding the company you are investing in. You need to know if the company is working on the right products and services. Understand the industry of the company. See if they are developing new products, technology, or services. Remember that whatever the company does affects the price of the stock. The best way for you to do this is to learn more about the company through fundamental analysis. You should always read the news about the company too. It is only this way that you can assess how well the company is doing. If you have any knowledge about the company or the products, you should spend some time to see where the company is heading.

When you start looking at a company, you need to ensure that you obtain the information from the right sources. Read this information carefully to understand whether the company is doing well or not. Ensure that the sources you use to obtain this information are reliable. If you get a fax, tip, or email from a person stating that one company is better than the rest, you need to make sure that you do not rush into investing. Take some time out and read about the company. Never invest in any company simply because of some information you may have received. Always conduct thorough research before you invest in the company. This is the only way you will learn if the company is doing well or not. Never waste your time or money. So, always stick to reliable sources and use that information to invest in the correct stocks.

Don't Trust Mails

You mustn't trust any emails that come from companies that claim to have enough knowledge about the stocks of other companies. These emails will also suggest the stocks that you should invest in, but the information in those emails is untrue. Companies cannot go through their investors' portfolios and suggest which stocks they should invest in. Even if a company does choose to do this, they may give you a suggestion that will not work for you. So, it is good to avoid these stocks and only invest in those stocks that you have all the information about.

Understand the Corrections

Remember that the price of stocks will be corrected in the market, and it is important that you remain patient. The price of the stock will drop when the market is correcting the price of the stocks in the market. If you are impatient, you will make a mistake and lose a lot of money. Always look at the company and make the right decisions about your investments. If a stock is either overpriced or underpriced, it means that the corrections will be made soon. Never sell your stocks in a panic and wait for the corrections to be made. You need to follow the news regularly, so you understand how or why the correction is being made.

Hire a Broker Only If Necessary

You should never hire a broker to do the job for you unless you need one. The only reason is that a broker will charge you a fee for helping you with your investments. They will also ask you to pay a commission, which will eat into your profits. You also need to remember that you need to pay your broker a fee regardless of whether you make a profit. So, they do not have to work hard to ensure that you make a profit. There are theories that companies hire brokers to increase the price of the stock in the market. They request the brokers to motivate investors to trade in a specific stock even if they do not want to invest in that stock. You will purchase these stocks if you can be swayed easily, which will lead to huge losses. You should always look for discounts online and see if you can trade independently. Avoid depending on your broker to buy and sell your stock.

Diversify Your Risks

This has been mentioned repeatedly across the book, so you can imagine how important it is for you to do this. You must always diversify your risks depending on the type of investment you make. This holds for any instrument. When you choose to invest in stocks, try to invest in stocks from different industries and sectors. If you invest in stocks only in one sector, you will lose a lot of money if the industry were to crash. It is because of this that you need to ensure that you diversify your capital. You must invest in different instruments in the market. Yes, one industry may be doing well compared to other industries, but this does not mean that you put all your money on stocks in that industry.

Money Movement

If you notice a sudden change in the price movement and the flow of money in the company, you know that the stock value will increase. If there is a sudden increase in the capital through external sources or it pumped its profits into its business, then it means that the company wants to expand. This will mean that the stock prices will rise, and it will benefit you as an investor. You must always keep track of the news and make the right decisions.

Look at the Stock Volume

If you notice that the volume of the stock has suddenly changed in the market, it is always a good idea to invest in that stock. The sudden changes in the price and volume of the stock will happen when there is some information in the news about the stock that makes people buy or sell stocks. Ensure that you capitalize on these situations so that you can make a huge profit. According to Timothy Sykes, you should always purchase a stock if you experience a high price after one year. The price of the stock will change only when the company talks about its earnings and bonuses.

Chapter 10. Advice to Minimizing Losses and Maximizing Gains

Some firms have different shares on the market. Some are good, and others are not so lucrative. How are you going to pick the right companies' stocks to make a full profit?

Well, the question is a million dollars one, but the answer is pretty easy. Before and unless you know the stock market, the answer to the million-dollar question cannot be sought. Yeah, business awareness is a must for anyone who wants to invest in stocks.

The good news is that trading on the Internet is very easy and hassle-free. All can invest in the stock at any time. Unlike other investment options on the market, there is no lock-in duration and restrictions.

However, you have to do some simple work in this sort of investment. At first, you will certainly reap the rewards of your investment if you prepare correctly and acquire ample knowledge of the workings of the stock market.

When the initial groundwork has been done, the answer to the million-dollar question can be sought. If a corporation issued public stock on the market — you bought those stocks, for instance, 100 shares at $10 each. Now, what factors will affect the price of the share? First and foremost, we must know why a specific company issues the public shares — the main purpose of shares issuance is to raise money for business expansion or pay the debt if any, and with the business increasing, the share prices often increase accordingly.

On the other hand, if you buy a share of a company and the share price falls in a few days, the company's growth curve is decreasing. Expert professionals, therefore, often recommend that investors keep an eye on major shares in the company.

Even if you have no idea what a company is, you can access information about a company, its growth curve, and its credibility in the previous industry. Many professionals recommend that they even purchase small-scale shares for full benefit.

Whenever you plan to buy a company share — gather all of the company's profile details and other important information. Following the study, purchase certain shares if you agree that a certain company share price will increase.

What Other Factors Affect the Trading Process?

Well, the website of the stock trading organization, the stockbroker, and the decision-making capacity impact the entire trading mechanism directly. It is always often easier to make a thorough market analysis on the Internet and then select the best alternative. If your fundamentals are simple, your investment will certainly give you maximum benefit. It is easier to do some simple work and then trade instead of jumping straight on the market. Now it is clear that professionals who make money on the same market have done all the required work required before the trade. So if you are a new investor and want to earn profits in a short time, first do your primary job, advise financial experts and then start trading online. Save money and build a good financial reserve to help your family better and effectively.

Options Trading — Losing Before Winning

Many options traders were frustrated when they set options to make a profit faster. Currently, nearly 90 % of the time, your options role will lose a lot until it would ultimately gain if it's raining at all. Sounds like something you've experienced?

Yeah, this is a reality of options trading and practice that seasoned traders like me learned to embrace. Many of my positions, especially single directional ones such as a long call, actually fall into a 60% loss until they eventually return to an astounding 100% profit. Yeah, most beginners took the loss early and missed the benefit.

What is the explanation for this phenomenon?

There are three key reasons why MOST options strategies lose a lot before making a profit.

The bid/work distribution of all the options involved in one position is first and foremost. The difference between the demand price and bid price of the options contract is the bid differential. Traders purchase retail options at the requested price and sell at the sale price.

An Options Contract with a $0.90 demand price and a $0.60 offer price has a $0.30 bid transaction range. This means that if you sell the option right as you purchased it, you instantly lose $0.30. The range of requests for options is considerably large for most inventories with spreads of $0.30 and spreads of up to $0.50 in some cases.

Only in extremely liquid inventories such as the QQQQ are there spreads of $0.10. Buying out money options costing about $0.70 with a bid of $0.20 could make you lose up to 30% right when you're in a spot! This is where most beginner options traders freak out, particularly if they commit the greatest sin of options trading—put all of their money into one trading.

Secondly, none of us, either George Soros or Warren Buffett, are stock market wizards. None of us will be able to trade reliably and move the stock exactly as planned at the moment it was launched (day trading excluded because periods are very limited in day trading).

As Jim Kramer said, we should always gradually develop a role over days because we are not geniuses. Yeah, unfortunately, most of the time, the stock seems to be heading in the opposite direction the very moment you sell.

The explanation seems that most traders enter trade emotionally when the shopping is heavy, which is also the point at which the stock retreats somewhat because of the over-compensation or over-sale when purchasing put options or shortcuts.

Leveraging in options trading now works in both ways. If it makes money faster, it will lose money faster, even though the stock just marginally shifts towards your favor.

Thirdly, Feedback!

Yeah, for a certain number of contracts, most options brokers will charge a minimum of $10 per trade. For beginner traders who take very small jobs, $20 ($10 for purchases and $10 for sales) may make considerable losses, particularly when money options are purchased. Committees often greatly sacrifice nuanced techniques for alternatives with multiple legs, such as the Condor Spread.

Combine the offer for spread loss with a pullback into the market, because we're not geniuses, and you'll end up losing 60% or more the very day that you placed a stock option. Sad but true, such a drastic and rapid loss would ruin most policy losses.

That is why many traders take losses too early to see stock recovery, ultimately in the right direction. Yeah, most losses are taken before the expiry of certain options! From a recent report, 60% of all available options were shut down before expiry!

When we use options trading strategies with limited risk, we can restrict this risk to a sum that we fully expect a loss, and we can tolerate loss if the trade goes wrong. When we transact directional options, we place some small "bets" over some time, and each time, ensure that the total is small enough to lead to negligible losses if the trade goes badly.

When you traded in this way, strength and control will overpower your emotions in the face of almost an immediate 60% loss in directional options trading.

Holding control also enables non-geniuses like us to wait for the reserves where they would ideal are, as most inventories won't move the way we want them to instantly (neutral tactics for options are very different, as you would expect the inventory not to move.

If you embrace the fact that your next trade option will possibly lose money considerably before they can benefit, it means you can use only the money that you intend to lose from the beginning to have a holding power that increases your chance of winning considerably

Chapter 11. Tax Implication and How to Reduce Their Impact on Your Earnings

Ah, we come to our favorite subject, taxes! The objective in the stock market is to make money, and every time that you make money, you are going to find yourself in a position of having to pay taxes on it. Unfortunately, it's a reality we can't escape. You might delay it, but at some point, you're going to have to pay.

There are many different issues you need to be aware of when it comes to taxes. This isn't a tax advisory book, and you should consult an accountant to make sure you're doing everything right. However, we'll take a brief look at some of the main issues.

Capital Gains

Suppose that you hold an asset, and the price appreciates. If you sell it, you'll realize a capital gain — in other words, you made money. When you make money by selling appreciated assets, you owe capital gains tax. The important thing to consider is how long you held the asset.

If you held the asset for one year or less, this is a short-term capital gain. The bad news about this is short-term capital gains are considered ordinary income. That means you'll pay the regular income tax rate on your gain.

If you hold the asset for longer than a year, even if it's just a day, then it becomes a long-term capital gain.

For some reason, Congress has decided that they know that holding assets for an arbitrary period that they made up is better, and so long-term capital gains have very favorable tax rates. These are much lower than income tax rates.

The bottom line here is that you'll want to take into account how long you have held an asset (aka stocks) when selling.

If you are a long-term investor and planning to hold your investments until retirement, this means that you will be paying long-term capital gains taxes on your investments when you sell them off to get the money. Of course, if your retirement is in the distant future (more than ten years away), it's hard to say what the laws are going to be.

Dividend Income

The important thing to note about dividend income when considering taxes is that it's considered to be ordinary income. There isn't anything special to consider dividend income. The one exception is dividends paid by an MLP. That's because they aren't technically dividends and you're considered a "partner" in the business. In that case, you are able to deduct depreciation from your taxes. The company passes it on to the "partners." This has huge implications. Many investors in MLPs are able to enjoy their income from the investments virtually tax-free. It's a little complicated, so if you start putting money into MLPs, you'll want to consult an accountant. The company will be sending you the appropriate forms.

Individual Retirement Accounts

One of the advantages of individual retirement accounts or IRAs is that they allow investments to grow inside of them tax-free. You can utilize this to your advantage. One way to do so is to buy dividend stocks inside the IRA and then reinvest the dividends. That way, you can continually grow your account and grow it beyond the usual limitations.

Expenses

Deducting expenses related to your investment might be problematic. The IRS isn't too friendly when it comes to deducting expenses related to investing. There is one exception, and that is if you are a day trader. Then a day trader can deduct expenses like publications they read and all the computer equipment and software services that they sign up for. But if you are doing ordinary investing, that might be a hard sell.

One way to get around it is to set up a business to run your investing. Then have the business buy all the equipment and so forth. Of course, this will inject other complications into the situation, so you'll have to weigh the pros and cons in order to determine whether or not it's really worth the extra hassle. Quite frankly, in most cases, it's not going to be.

Understanding Your Brokerage Account and Statement

You'd be surprised to know that most extremely wealthy people have taxable brokerage accounts. It provides an avenue for them to benefit from the stock market and diversify their income stream. As we've discussed earlier in this book, if you want to invest huge amounts of money and be a successful investor, you have to open a taxable brokerage account.

What is a Brokerage Account?

A brokerage account is a taxable investment account that you can use to buy and sell stocks and other securities. As the name suggests, it's opened through a brokerage firm. It's much like a bank account. You have to deposit money into your account before you can start buying and selling stocks.

You can deposit money into your account through checks or electronic funds transfers. You can also wire money to your account.

Type of Investments a Brokerage Account Can Hold

Brokerage accounts are not just for stocks. There are a number of securities that a brokerage account can hold, including:

- **Common Stock** — This represents partial ownership of a company. It usually comes with voting rights.
- **Preferred stock** — This stock usually comes with high dividend payments, but it's more expensive than common stock. Preferred stock shareholders typically don't have any voting rights.
- **Bonds** — A bond is a debt security. When you purchase a bond, the issuer (usually a government entity) owes you money. You earn money from bonds through interest rates.
- **Mutual Fund** — A mutual fund is funded by different shareholders. It's basically a pool of money that's invested in different securities. It's relatively easy to invest in a mutual fund. Plus, it's usually managed by a financial professional. You can buy different mutual funds, too, so you don't have to put all your money into one mutual fund.

- **ETF** — An ETF, or Exchange Traded Fund, is a basket of different securities that are traded like a stock. An ETF is a good investment because it has trading flexibility. It helps you diversify your investment portfolio and manage risk. It's also cheaper than a traditional mutual fund.
- **REIT** — A real estate investment trust, or REIT, is a company that either finances or operates income-producing real estate properties, such as commercial buildings. REITs usually own various income-generating real estate companies, such as hospitals, warehouses, hotels, and malls. You can invest in publicly traded REITs using your brokerage account.
- **Money Market and Certificate of Deposit** — A money market account generally represents pools of liquid mutual funds. It has higher interest rates and has a limited check-writing capacity. A certificate of deposit is basically a time deposit. For example, you agree to deposit $10,000 into your account. You can't withdraw that amount for five years, but you'll earn an interest rate throughout this period. So, if you earn $1,000 in interest per year, you're going to earn an extra $5,000 for your deposit after five years.

Cash Brokerage Accounts and Margin Brokerage Accounts

There are two main brokerage account types — cash accounts and margin accounts. A cash brokerage account requires you to deposit cash into your account. You'll have to pay for your transactions in cash and in full when you have a cash brokerage account.

A margin account, on the other hand, allows you to borrow from the broker using some of your assets as collateral to buy securities.

If you're a beginner, it's best to go for a cash brokerage account. Why? Well, margin brokerage accounts are complex and will get you buried in debt if you're not careful.

Limits of Money You Can Deposit in a Brokerage Account

As previously mentioned, other investment plans such as the IRA and 401(k) have limits, but taxable brokerage accounts do not, so you can deposit and invest as much as you want. That said, keep in mind that you do have to pay taxes for this type of investment.

How Many Brokerage Accounts Can One Have?

You can have as many brokerage accounts as you want, but keep in mind that most brokerage firms require a minimum deposit amount of $500 to $2000, so opening multiple accounts can be costly.

However, if you have unlimited resources, you can open multiple accounts with different brokerage firms.

Difference between a Discount Broker and a Full-Service Broker

There are two general types of broker:

- A full-service broker and
- A discount broker

A full-service brokerage account is great because it comes with a dedicated broker. You can call, text, or email him should you want to make an order. This broker usually knows you personally, and sometimes he knows your family. He also knows your finances intimately. He's like a financial advisor. You usually have to meet him regularly to discuss your portfolio.

Full-service brokers usually charge high commission fees. A discount broker, on the other hand, doesn't charge much. But, this type of broker usually operates online. A discount brokerage account is like a Do It Yourself (DIY) investment plan.

So, what should you choose? Well, it depends on what your priority is. If you are on a budget and you really want to save money, it's best to open a discount brokerage account. But, if you really want to have a financial adviser, it's a great idea to open a full-service brokerage account.

Understanding Your Broker's Statement

A broker's statement is a monthly report that contains the activities in your brokerage account. You can choose to receive a paper statement, but you can usually just check it online as well.

It pays to examine your statement carefully so you can spot some kind of fraud. When you first receive your income statement, you have to check to see if it looks professional. An unprofessional-looking statement is a red flag. Legitimate brokerage firms invest time and effort to make sure that their reports look polished and professional.

Here's what you'll find in your broker statement:

- **Statement Period Date** — A broker's statement reports how your investment is doing at a specific period of time, usually a month. If you don't see a statement period date, that's a red flag.

- **Account Number, Account Name, and Address** — This obviously contains your taxable brokerage account number, your name, and your present address. Be worried if this information is incorrect.

- **Contact Information** — This contains the contact information of your broker. If you don't see this anywhere in the statement, the brokerage firm you're dealing with may be dubious.

- **Name of the Clearing Firm** — This contains the name and the contact number of the clearing firm that holds your investments. FINRA rules require brokerage firms to place this information in their statements. So, be alarmed if you don't see this anywhere in your statement.

- **Account Summary** — This provides insight with regards to how your account is doing. This can help you review and assess your investment decisions.

- **Fees** — This covers the transaction and commission fees you've paid within the time period.

- **Account Activity** — This is where you can see the stocks you've bought or sold within that particular time period.

- **Margin** — If you have a margin account, you'll find this section. This contains the amount you've borrowed to purchase stocks and other securities.

- **Portfolio Detail** — This section breaks down your investment by types like stocks, bonds, or mutual funds.

Chapter 12. What to Do and What to Buy in a Down Market

Now that you have an idea of why you need to invest and some fundamental principles in investment as well as asset classes, you can invest in it. For you to start winning in a big way, you would have to put in the time. You would have to put in the effort. You would have to have the proper experience and groundwork to make that happen. And in many cases, even with the best-laid plans and with the best strategies laid out, things still don't pan out.

The better approach is to do the best with the situation you are facing. In other words, use specific strategies that would enable you to position yourself to come out ahead. They might not necessarily result in you making tons of money or experiencing truly stupendous returns, but they can position you for solid gains. The following strategies enable you to do just that.

Buy Depressed Assets

Now, this might seem straightforward. After all, this is just a reiteration of the classic investment and commercial maxim of "buy low, sell high." However, the big challenge here is in determining what constitutes a "depressed asset."

You might be thinking that a stock that was trading at $50 and pops to $150 might not be all that depressed if it fell to $100. You might be thinking, where's the depression? This is not a fire sale. It hasn't fallen enough.

If you look at the stock's trajectory and how much growth potential and market attention, it might very well turn out that the stock is headed to $300. Do you see how this works?

If that's the case, then scooping up the stock at the price of $100 after it fell from $150 is a steal. After all, buying something worth $300 for a third of its price is one heck of a bargain.

Now, the big issue here is how do you know the stock's full future value? This is where serious analysis comes in. You can't just buy stocks on hype. It would be best if you looked at facts that would inform the growth trajectory of that stock.

For example, is it a market leader? Does it have certain drugs in the approval pipeline that have little to no competition? Is it on the cusp of a breakthrough drug patent? Is it in the process of buying out its competition?

There are many factors that you should consider, which can impact the overall future value of a stock. You should pay attention to its current developments, and you should pay attention to the news cycle surrounding the company.

You should also pay attention to its industry. Is its industry fast-expanding, or is it a "sunset industry" on its last legs? If it's in a sunset industry, there might still be opportunities there because, usually, such industries witness a tremendous amount of consolidation. Whatever the case may be, always be on the lookout for the future value of a stock based on what you know now, as well as its past performance.

Dollar-Cost Averaging

What happens if you buy a stock that subsequently crashes? This happens to the very best of us. If this happened to you, don't get depressed. Don't think that you suck at investing. Don't think that all is lost. If you get caught in a downturn, it might be an amazing opportunity.

Now, it's important to note that almost all stocks experience a pullback. I have yet to come across a stock that has appreciated positively with no dips in its trading history. I'm not aware of a stock that hasn't experienced a day-to-day dip in pricing. All stocks experience a pullback. Even stocks that are well on their way to becoming breakthrough or high-valued stocks will experience dips.

What happens if you bought a stock that drops in value tremendously? Well, you have two options at this point. You can wait for the stock to keep going up and then start buying some more. You're taking bets on its recovery.

The better approach would be to use this as an opportunity. For example, if you bought, for the sake of simplicity, one share of stock at $100 a share, and the price crashes 50% to $50 a share, you can buy one share at $50, and this would average out your holdings to $75 per share.

Ideally, you should wait for the stock to drop so much and then buy a whole lot. This enables you to set your break-even point at a much lower level. For example, using the same hypothetical facts mentioned above, instead of buying one share, you buy 9 shares at $50. So, what happens is, the average price per share gets reduced to $55.

Even if the depressed stock manages to limp along and possibly pop up here and there, it doesn't have to pop up all that much to get all your money back from your position because once it hits $55, you're at break-even territory. Compare this with breaking even at $75 or, worse yet, waiting for the stock to come back to $100 a share. It's anybody's guess whether it will back to that level.

This strategy is called dollar-cost averaging, and it is very useful. You must have free cash available, and you must use that free cash at the right time.

That's how you maximize its value. That's how you fully take advantage of opportunities that present themselves. Otherwise, you might be in a situation where the stock crashes so hard that you could have broken even very easily with little money spent, but unfortunately, you were locked out because you don't have the cash to do it.

Buy Self Liquidating Assets

Another investing strategy you can take is to buy assets that pay for themselves. For example, if you spent a million dollars buying a building, but the building generates rents totaling $100,000 per year, the building pays for itself in roughly 13 years or more, factoring in taxes and other costs.

Self-liquidating assets may seem too good to be true, but they are very real. Most of this applies to certain types of real estate, like commercial properties. However, this strategy also applies to stocks and bonds.

For example, if you buy stocks that have no dividend and you buy bonds, you can use the bond interest to start paying off your stock's portfolio. Of course, this can take quite a bit of time if you factor in interest rates as well as taxes.

Smart Money Valuation

Another winning strategy is to buy into private corporations as a sophisticated investor at a much lower valuation. Now keep in mind that many mobile app companies are popping up all over the United States. You don't necessarily have to live in Silicon Valley of California to have access to these types of companies.

The great thing about these companies is that in the beginning, they require very little capital. Many require "Angel," "per-Angel," or even raw seed capital. The founder would have a rough idea of software, an app, or a website. This is the most basic stage of a company's evolution.

Now, when you come in as a source of seed capital, you can lock into a large chunk of the company's stock for a very low valuation. For example, somebody comes up with a startup idea, and the initial cost is a maximum of $1 million. If you were to invest $250,000, you have a 25% stake in the company.

You may be thinking that 25% of a company that's not worth that much, which is very, very risky, doesn't seem like a winning proposition. Well, keep in mind that after the seed stage, the company's valuation usually goes up. So, once your money has been used to push the company further along its developmental path, the company's valuation starts to go up, especially if they now have something more concrete to show other investors.

You may be asking yourself, okay, the smart money valuation thing sounds awesome. This is great in theory, but is it real? How can the Average Joe investor get in on such deals?

There are websites like Angel List and others, as well as LinkedIn groups that publicize startup projects that are actively recruiting investors. Of course, you need to do your homework and pay attention to the track record of the founders.

Chapter 13. How to Use Both Macroeconomic and Microeconomic Analysis

You can't go to war without a weapon. You can't just buy a stock; you must do extensive research. You must learn to be your own stock analyst. This will help you make wise and sound investment decisions.

To do comprehensive stock research, you must apply two methods used in economics—microeconomics analysis and macroeconomic analysis.

Macro-Economic Analysis

As discussed earlier in this book, economic forces (such as the law of supply and demand) affect stock prices. So, before you invest in a stock, you have to use a top-down global research approach. You must look at the global trends. You must look at the big picture.

As of this writing, Airbnb is not a public company yet, but for the purpose of discussion, let's assume that it is. A lot of cities in Europe and in the United States have banned Airbnb, but it continues to grow in various cities in the world. In fact, you can find a lot of great Airbnb deals in Bali, Malaysia, Singapore, Zurich, Mykonos, and Faro. Plus, it still has a number of untapped markets. If you look at the big picture, you'll see that Airbnb is still a great investment because of its huge growth potential.

Aside from looking at the company's global overview, you must also consider other factors, such as:

Interest Rates

When the interest rate is high, it would be more costly for companies and individuals to pay their debts. This decreases their disposable income and their spending. This also affects business revenues and can drive down the stock prices.

But, when a country has a low-interest rate, people have more disposable income. They'll end up buying more stuff. This could lead to an increase in stock prices.

However, you have to take note that rising interest rates can benefit specific industries, such as the financial sector — banks, mortgage companies, lending companies, and insurance companies.

The Cyclical Nature of an Industry

Before you buy a company's stock, you have to determine if that company belongs to a cyclical industry.

Cyclical sectors such as the automobile industry and the construction industry are sensitive to the ups and downs of the economy. When the economy is good, their prices go up, but they go down when there's a recession.

Try to avoid investing in companies in cyclical sectors (unless you're very good at timing your investments). You'd want to invest in a stock that can withstand economic setbacks.

Stock Market Index

As previously discussed, an index tracks the performance of market leaders. So, in essence, it reflects the overall health of the stock market. If an index is trending up, it means that stock market players are a bit optimistic and a bull market may be happening.

Industry-Wide Research

Let's say that you want to invest in luxury brands such as Louis Vuitton (LVMH) or YSL. Before you do that, you must look into the overall health of that industry.

If you look closely, you might discover that luxury brands are not doing as well as they used to be because of online shops and China-made products.

Micro- Economic Analysis

When you do macro-economic analysis, you are looking at the economy and the industry, but understand that microeconomic analysis uses a "bottom-up" approach. This means that you have to do extensive company research.

You have to look into the different aspects of the company, such as:

- **The Company's Product** — Is the product good? Does it have loyal customers? Is the product going to be relevant ten years from now? Let's say that a music store is selling its stocks. Would you buy it? Well, let's face it: no one buys CDs anymore. We just download music from the internet or check YouTube. Technology is changing by the minute. A widely used product may become irrelevant and unnecessary in the next few years. Just look at what happened to diskettes.
- **Sales and Revenue** — Are the company earning money? Are their products doing well in the market?
- **Debt to Equity Ratio** — Is the company's debt bigger than its equity? If so, then you should run as fast as you can.

- **P/E Ratio** — If the company has a high P/E ratio, it means that it has high growth potential. However, it also means that the stock is overvalued. A low P/E ratio means that the company has low growth potential, but it also means that it's overvalued. If you're into growth investing, choose a company with a high P/E ratio. But you have to choose a company with a low P/E ratio if you're into value investing.
- **Earnings per Share (EPS)** — A company with high EPS is really doing well. It's profitable. So, assuming other factors check out (e.g. it's not using a lot of unsustainable debt to generate the earnings), it's a good idea to invest in a company with a high EPS.
- **Company Management** — Do you trust the people managing the company? Do they engage in unethical business practices? If you don't trust the people running the company, then avoid it at all costs.

Also, make sure that the company's profit has been trending upward at least in the last five years.

Chapter 14. How to Create a Secure Financial Future

In today's scenario, where the economy hides and seeks some sort of position, financial security is a must for every individual. Although it is a broad category, financial security, however, means investment and income in the future. Look at the market, and you'll find different options for investment. Often it's hard to pick the right option.

Trading is yet another investment opportunity that offers no limits, unlike other investment strategies, but just good returns. However, as we all know, the stock market is a constantly changing environment, and we need technical analysis to learn from it; that will ensure your market success.

Unfortunately, many of us are not going to analyze it and continue to invest. The result is obvious, and that is why people often do not respond disproportionately to stock trading.

On the other hand, many of us profit from the same market, but attitudes and strategies differ. Why is one person a successful trader and another failing trader? If you know the difference in this small line, your investment strategy is guaranteed to succeed. Before you start trading, there are many things to consider:

- **Financial Strength** — Firstly, your financial strength — how much you want to invest — must be analyzed. You can start with small funds if you are a new trader. You can add more funds to your investment plan once you make money.
- **Experts in Finance** — investment is not a simple task. Proper planning is, therefore, a must. If you know market trends and trading experience, you can plan without assistance. However, if you are new and

would like some assistance, please consult financial experts — they are available online and offer the best investment plan.
- **Comprehensive Market Knowledge** — A successful trader needs good market knowledge.
- **Online Stock Broke** — Because we are unable to trade directly, your broker makes all forms of trading and charges a small fee in return. It's like a connection between the trader and the stock market. You should therefore have a good broker who can also give you advice and let you know about the most profitable company shares.
- **Technical Analysis** — A complete competitive market analysis is a must. You have to analyze stock price trends in the last 3 to 5 days, and you can predict market mood further. This research, however, does not always succeed; it still gives us an idea of the market.
- **Positive Attitude** — it is not your attitude; it is your business attitude. Those who often see the market as a risky forum affect many of us and create a negative business attitude. In that very case, you can make the wrong decision, even if you are on the right track. Therefore, you must be optimistic and try to believe in yourself.

One of the main factors for successful trading is the ability to understand the market and to adapt to changing circumstances. Once you get to know the market moods, you can better reap the advantages. Invest now and build a strong future financial reserve.

How to Choose the Right Stocks to Invest In

Mia worked in a software development company for fifteen years. She's good at her job, but she was always stressed and tired. So, she decided to give stock market investment a try in order to build a passive income portfolio that would help her retire early. She met with an old friend named Kate, a financial analyst. Kate helped her invest in high-quality and fast-growing stocks.

After two years, Mia had earned $650,000 capital appreciation profit. She quit her job and traveled around the world. She soon used part of her earnings to establish her own graphic design company. Her $650,000 grew to over $2 million.

Mia is living her dream life. She owns her time. She has a successful business, and she even bought a beach house in Miami.

Chloe was Mia's former colleague. Like Mia, she's been working in the software development industry for about fifteen years. She was also tired. After she heard about Mia's success, she decided to invest in stocks, too.

Chloe didn't know anything about the stock market and didn't know how to choose the right stocks. She invested in companies that were buried in debt and engaged in unethical business practices. So, she ended up losing $10,000.

A lot of people get rich through stock market investment, but many people lose huge amounts of money too. This is the reason why you should be careful in choosing the right stocks to invest in. You have to be clear about your investment goals and use the right strategies that work for you and match your risk tolerance level. You must also do extensive research before you place your bet on a stock.

Setting an Investment Objective

Before you start investing, you should be clear about what your investment objectives are. You should also decide what type of investor you want to be. Do you want to be a long-term investor? Or, do you want to be a day trader, trading stocks by the minute?

You must be clear about what you want to achieve through stock market investing. How much are you willing to invest? How much do you want to earn each year? What are you willing to risk?

You need to set financial goals like how much you want to earn in one year or in five years. You should also set non-financial goals. Why? Well, your investment earnings are just mere tools that you can use to support your non-financial goals. So, what do you want to achieve? Do you want to have a grand wedding? Do you want to travel to a foreign country at least twice a year?

Factors to Consider in Choosing a Stock

The key to building a profitable investment portfolio is choosing the right stocks. When you're starting, buying individual stocks is costlier than investing in low-cost mutual funds. Below are the factors that you should consider in choosing stocks to invest in.

- **Growth in Earnings**

Before you invest in a company, you should check its earnings and make sure that it's consistently growing over time. The growth doesn't have to be huge. You just have to look for an upward trend in earnings.

For example, let's say that you have an extra $3,000 and you want to invest it in stock. You're looking to invest in two companies. Company A is one of the biggest steel manufacturers in the country, while Company B produces the nation's best-selling batteries.

Take time to examine the data below:

- **Company A: Leading Steel Manufacturer**

Year	Earnings
2005	$2,158,111,202
2006	$2,160,369,000
2007	$2,080,250,000

2008	$1,988,910,000
2009	$1,888,630,121
2010	$1,780,980,011
2011	$1,761,918,870
2012	$1,709,919,450
2013	$1,670,980,689
2014	$1,659,658,905
2015	$1,640,050,814
2016	$1,590,010,110
2017	$1,550,000,289

2018	$1,499,110,980

- **Company B: Leading Battery Manufacturer**

Year	Earnings
2005	$750,000,905
2006	$805,963,960
2007	$815,750,690
2008	$909,530,066
2009	$915,784,210
2010	$918,974,560
2011	$990,741,632

2012	$1,101,890,390
2013	$1,156,120,450
2014	$1,190,110,000
2015	$1,220,000,980
2016	$1,240,780,360
2017	$1,310,000.550
2018	$1,399,222,080

If you look closely, you'll see that Company A has a lot more earnings than Company B. However, its revenue has been declining since 2008. This means that the company is facing problems. It could be mismanagement or a decreasing market share due to an aggressive competitor entering the space.

Company B, on the other hand, has had steady growing earnings since 2006. This company is doing something right and is more worthy of your hard-earned money.

- **Stability**

Sir Tim Berners-Lee published a paper about a proposed information management program called the "internet" in 1989. He then implemented the first successful communication between a Hypertext Transfer Protocol (HTTP) and a server a few months later.

In 1990, Berners-Lee began writing the World Wide Web (www) — the first-ever web browser. The next year, he launched the first-ever web page. This forever changed the world. This is what stock market players call a black swan.

According to risk analyst Nassim Nicholas Taleb, a black swan is an event that's hard to predict that can forever change the world. And if you're wise enough to predict or at least spot a black swan at its early stage, you're going to win big in the stock market and in business. This explains why early internet entrepreneurs like Jack Ma and Jeff Bezos are extremely wealthy.

And soon, promising internet companies decided to go public and the investors went crazy placing their eggs in the "internet business basket."

But after the tech industry got a little too crowded and the world experienced a stock market crash in 2008, the revenues of internet companies became volatile. So, a lot of investors ended up losing huge amounts of money.

Even so, this is just an example. It doesn't mean that you shouldn't invest in the tech industry. All companies are bound to lose their stock value at some point, especially during periods of recession and economic crisis.

To achieve long-term success in the stock market, you have to invest in companies that are strong and stable enough to endure unfavorable economic conditions. Erratic stock price fluctuation is not a good sign.

To illustrate this point, look at the graph below:

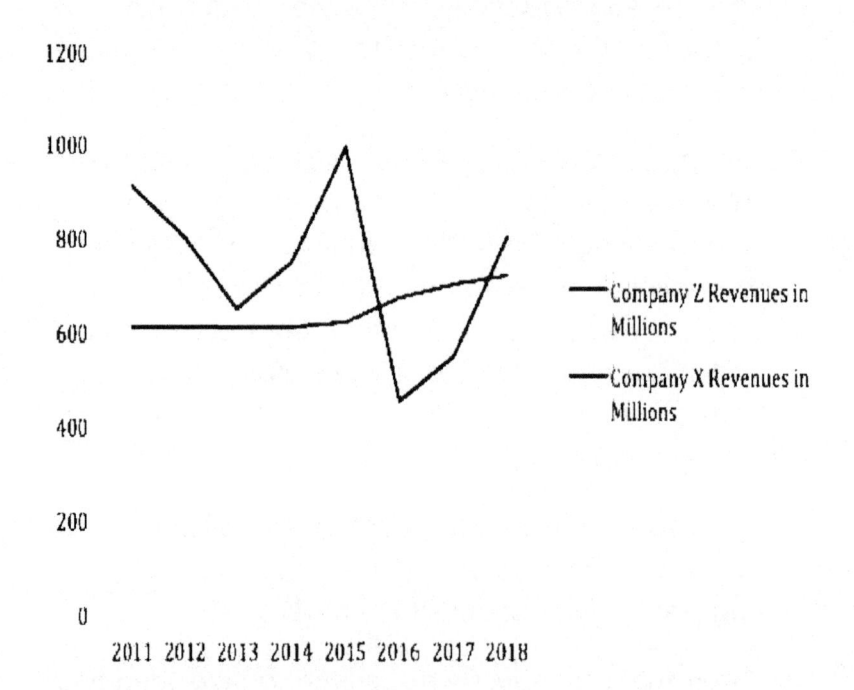

Notice that Company Z's revenue doesn't fluctuate as much as Company X's. This means that it's more stable and a good choice for long-term investment.

Chapter 15. Stock Market Strategies for Profitable Investing

Learning how to use successful bond market strategies will vary between the loss and possible profits of all your hard-earned money. These tips help you find the right investment strategies to use and avoid those that harm you more.

The Business Know

It is necessary to know the market before you can begin investment so that you can better understand how to use effective stock market strategies. Study the market as best as you can, including those stocks that are of interest to you — there are plenty of websites and other reference material that can help you get an understanding of the market.

Besides, partnering with a reputable financial advisor or creditable financial information provider is a perfect stock market strategy to understand better the market and what it can do for you.

Evite Fraud

Beginners are particularly vulnerable to fraud and schemes designed to draw prospective investors to divide their hard-playing cash. Many who fall for these sly stock market schemes won't do anything; in fact, only the scammers themselves profit from these scams!

The bottom line — most definitely if it sounds too good to be true. Equipped with the right investment strategies and expertise, you won't fall into these enticing schemes.

A Stock Broker Notice

An investment plan is a perfect way to use a stockbroker as a reliable broker will help you to decide on your portfolio and help you pick the right stock for your situation. A trustworthy broker can use his expertise to help you gain greater market knowledge, including trends, stock growth, and whether to buy or sell.

Furthermore, a stockbroker can show you even better investment strategies than you can buy. A reliable broker will happily assist you with your investments and will do everything possible to lead you in the right direction.

Learning how to play the stock market can be terrifying for beginning investors in particular. By learning about the market, avoiding schemes that are too good for you to be true, and finding a reputable stockbroker, you will learn successful stock market strategies to make your investment profitable.

It is crucial for beginners to have a solid understanding of the market and how to be as effective as possible before even beginning to invest in the stock market. The following bonds will lead you in the right direction.

Train Yourself

The first step towards being a good investor is to educate you. Take a few lessons in accounting, read as many books on investment as possible, and look online for different facets of the business and how it works for you.

Another suggestion that helps you become a better investor is to talk to a licensed stockbroker or financial advisor. A renowned advisor can provide you with direct personal information which you are not able to find in books or posts, and can also sit one-on-one with you and answer all your questions.

Take Stock Exchange Tools

Another smart tip is to use apps for some tasks. It is advisable to invest in personal finance software that can help you handle your money and track income and losses. A program that helps you monitor your stock market portfolio and trace when to buy or sell will be another software to consider; evaluate potential profits vs. risks of a specific stock, and track stock prices.

Continue to Train

One of the best investment tips, particularly for beginners, is to continue to practice until you have a good understanding of the market and its concepts. If you do not follow some other bond suggestion, it should certainly be a priority, regardless of what.

Many stock simulation programs, without taking risks and investing, will make you experience the real thing. Some of these systems are more practical than others, but all of them help you understand the idea of stock purchasing and trading.

Chapter 16. COVID-19 Effects on Working with Stocks

The stock market's reaction to the COVID-19 pandemic and the subsequent economic fallout has raised both fears and questions. This column delves into unexpected developments. There is evidence that shareholders favored the less distressed companies, and that credit facilities and government guarantees, lower policy interest rates, and stock price lockdowns helped to minimize the stock price decline. Fundamentals, on the other hand, only account for a limited portion of stock market fluctuations at the country level. Overall, it's difficult to argue that the correlations between stock prices and fundamentals have been shaky at best.

The World Health Organization (WHO) declared on June 8, 2020, that the COVID-19 pandemic was worsening around the world and cautioned against complacency: "the majority of people worldwide are still vulnerable to infection. "...With more than six months left in the pandemic, now is not the time for any nation to ease up on the gas." The US stock market started its fourth consecutive week of gains on the same day. The S&amp P 500 index has returned to where it was at the start of 2020, erasing the historical decline (one-third of its value) that occurred between February 20 and March 23, 2020, as if nothing had happened. As seen in the graph, this is absolutely unparalleled.

Is there something unusual about the stock market behavior during COVID-19? The reaction of financial markets poses serious concerns as the world suffers from the worst economic crisis since the Great Depression (Baldwin and Weder di Mauro 2020a, 2020b, Bénassy-Quéré and Weder di Mauro 2020, Coibon et al. 2020). Stock prices have been wildly fluctuating since the start of the crisis. They dismissed the pandemic at first, then panicked as it spread to Europe. They are now acting as if the millions of people who have been poisoned, the 400,000 deaths, and the containment of half the world's population has had no economic effects.

Paul Krugman (2020) said out loud what many people were thinking in one of his famous New York Times columns: "Whenever you consider the economic ramifications of stock prices, you want to remember three rules." To begin with, the stock market is not the same as the economy. Second, the stock market isn't the same thing as the economy. Third, the stock market is not a replacement for the economy (...). The correlation between stock performance and real economic growth, which is largely driven by the oscillation between greed and fear, has always been shaky at best. "Malkiel and Shiller (2020)," two other well-known economists, have also discussed the stock market's strange conduct in the face of the pandemic. The suspected stock market irrationality, according to Malkiel, is just "apparent," and the COVID-19 crisis does not "imply that markets are dysfunctional" since there are no arbitrage possibilities and stock markets remain difficult to beat. "Speculative prices can statistically mimic a random walk, but they are not as bound to genuine knowledge (...), says Shiller. The infectious stories about the coronavirus had their own internal complexities that were only tangentially linked to the truth."

What lessons can be learned about stock market actions from the COVID-19 crisis? This debate is particularly important for financial economists, but it is also important because the general public has a negative perception of stock markets, which should worry us (Rajan 2015) —

especially after the COVID-19 crisis placed science and 'experts' to the test (Aksoy et al. 2020), without sparing economists.

A rapidly growing body of research looking at stock market reactions to the COVID-19 pandemic is already providing some insights. Although the stock market's actions during the pandemic could seem spontaneous, irrational, or even insane at first glance, closer observation shows that they did not respond randomly. Several studies have shown that stock markets are effective at discounting the most vulnerable companies: those that are financially fragile, vulnerable to international value chain disruption, vulnerable to corporate social responsibility, or less resilient to social distancing (Alburque et al. 2020, Ding et al. 2020, Fahlenbrach et al. 2020, Pagano et al. 2020, Ramelli and Wagner 2020). Furthermore, it appears that, at least in the medium term, stock market declines are linked to analyst forecast revisions (Landier and Thesmar 2020). We approach these papers from a macroeconomic standpoint. While the studies described above provide useful details, some questions remain unanswered.

What has been the response of the stock market to the COVID-19 pandemic? How do we understand the disparities in responses around countries? Are there any macroeconomic or institutional factors that influence stock market response across countries, and if so, which ones? Are these disparities the product of how governments treated the pandemic? How have financial markets responded to nationwide lockdowns and economic policies aimed at 'flattening' the curves of infection and recession? (2020 Gourinchas)

We discuss how stock markets have incorporated public knowledge about the COVID-19 pandemic and subsequent lockdowns in our recent paper (Capelle-Blancard and Desroziers 2020). Despite the fact that the COVID-19 shock was global, not all countries were affected in the same way, and they did not react in the same way. This high heterogeneity is something we take advantage of. We want to understand the differences in stock market responses by looking at the situation in each country prior to the crisis, as well as the subsequent containment measures (social distancing and stay-at-home orders) and economic policies (fiscal and monetary) that were introduced during the crisis. From January to April 2020, we consider a panel of 74 nations, which can be divided into four phases: incubation, outbreak, fear, and rebound. We gathered regular data on stock index prices, COVID-19 total cases and deaths, global market sentiment and volatility, government responses to the outbreak, and various indicators of mobility for each region (or lack thereof).

Three main results emerge about stock market reactions during the COVID-19 pandemic. First, after initially ignoring the pandemic (until February 21, 2020), financial markets responded strongly to the rise in the number of infected people in each country (February 23 to March 20, 2020), with volatility increasing as fears about the pandemic increased. Following central bank intervention (23 March to 20 April 2020), however, news of the health crisis no longer seemed to bother shareholders, and shares rebounded all over the world. Second, it appears that country-specific characteristics had little, if any, impact on stock market responses. Stock markets in countries more vulnerable to the pandemic did not respond as strongly, either because of systemic economic fragility (for example, indebted countries) or because of exposure to transmission vectors (for example, countries with 'at-risk' populations). Third, the number of COVID-19 cases in neighboring (but mostly wealthy) countries piqued investors' interest. Fourth, the fall in stock prices was mitigated by credit facilities and government guarantees, lower policy interest rates, and lockout measures.

Finally, do capital markets take into account all available information? In fact, we can see the glass as either half-full or half-empty. On the one hand, the stock market's behavior during the COVID-19 pandemic is not entirely coincidental. Our research indicates that the reaction of stock markets was affected by health policies introduced during the crisis to restrict virus transmission and macroeconomic policies aimed at supporting businesses, rather than the situation of countries prior to the crisis. Fundamentals, on the other hand, only account for a (very) small portion of stock market volatility. It's difficult to deny that the connection between stock prices and fundamentals has been anything but loose, as Krugman and Shiller have claimed.

Conclusion

There are also many different types of investments, orders, and such that the individual may make. It is crucial that the investor knows the differences between these and can decide on which methods the investor wishes to invest in. However, the investor must know the pros and cons of each to reach that conclusion. The investor must educate himself or herself before making any further decisions on their investments and strategies for trading. There are many elements of the stock market that one must familiarize themselves with; the more that you know, the better the chance of you receiving a high return on your investment is.

Stock market investing can be very powerful for any person looking to create wealth or build a side income. Among all the asset classes, stock investments have generated the best returns historically. Consequently, it is beneficial for you over the long term that you develop a sound understanding of this highly profitable investment avenue.

The next step is to follow this through and begin your quest as a stock investor. It is important to begin by setting goals for yourself as an investor. You must consider all of the variables involved in investing. Setting goals will help provide you with a sense of direction. By using this as a reference, you may decide on which path of investing you will choose. What will be the time period of your investment? Will you purchase individual stocks or ETFs? How much risk are you willing to take in your investments? These questions, among others, must be answered to provide you with clear goals in your investing. After this, you may create an account, fund your account, and start trading. There must be research done, and you must select your stocks. After this, you are on the path to success in trading.

After you have accomplished this, you must continue to conduct research on the market, monitor your stocks, and manage your portfolio. Being an investor is an ongoing process. This can really help you to get started in learning about stock, and it may serve as a reference guide throughout your stock investing career. There will constantly be changes in the economy, the stock market will fluctuate every day, and the stocks themselves will continuously move. However, the basic concepts of stock will always be helpful to know, and this provides its readers with those basics that are necessary for one to be successful in stock investing.

The goal is to help investors, especially those who are just getting started with investing in the stock market, to learn the basic concepts of the stock market that will help them to initiate the trading process and become both successful and profitable in their investments.

Stock investing requires discipline, patience, and thoughtful analysis. Diversification is an essential strategy for successful stock investing. Keeping your emotions in check is also a crucial part of becoming a successful investor. A long-term approach to stock investments provides many times good returns.

By reading it to the end, you are proving that you are disciplined and ready to work hard! Many rookie investors spend their money investing blindly. Unlike the majority, you have taken your time to acquire knowledge to make wise decisions. Good job!

DAY TRADING SWING & FOREX FOR BEGINNERS

A CRASH COURSE TO INVEST IN THE STOCK MARKET:

MAKING A LIVING BY BUYING AND SELLING STOCKS, OPTIONS AND CURRENCIES,

AND USING PASSIVE INCOME STRATEGIES

Introduction

It is near impossible to predict market movements, and that is why day traders, swing traders, and forex traders place trades of any length in which they take a position with the hope that the price will move favorably for them. Day trading, swing trading, and forex trading can all be profitable in the long term if done correctly. Give one or more of these strategies a try!

Day Trading

Day trading involves making short-term trades on assets such as stocks or currencies with the goal of making a quick profit when you buy an asset and sell it at a higher price before its value decreases. To do this, day traders generally enter a position and then exit it if the price does not move in their favor. In the long term, day trading can be profitable for traders who know what to do to make correct trades at optimal times and avoid losing money due to falls in the stock market. Day trading can be very high risk, and taking excessive risks can lead to devastating losses over time.

Swing Trading

Swing trading involves taking a position in an asset over a longer period of time (ranging from days to years). When a swing trader first enters a trade, it is called a long position because they will be holding the asset for some time. If the price does not go up or down in their favor, they will be happy with their profit or loss. But if the price increases significantly by the end of the time frame, then they are considering taking an opposite position by selling the shares or contracts at that point. This strategy takes more effort and can take more than one year to make money, but it also has less risk than day trading.

Forex Trading

Forex trading involves buying and selling currencies. The market is open 24 hours a day, so it is possible to trade on the short-term fluctuations in the market. Just as with stocks, currencies can be more volatile than others at times. A successful forex trader should be able to identify trends, determine their risk tolerance and time frame for trades, manage risks accordingly, and be able to stick with a plan through thick and thin.

Day Trading VS. Forex Trading VS. Swing Trading

Before I go any further, let me define what these terms mean. The most basic concept is that they refer to the same groups of conditions. But to be clear, Forex involves currency trading; day trading involves the buying and selling of stocks or futures; swing trading involves both stocks and futures.

The average Forex trade takes about 40-60 days to make money on a short-term basis (2-4 weeks). It might take even longer if the market is moving too fast or if it's in a tight range for too long. A long-term trend will generally move at a faster pace than short-term trends.

If you are going to day trade, then I recommend day trading the trend. Always trade what the trend is doing. I can make more money on a trend than on a range, and while I was trading in one of my previous blogs, I had a 15-year streak of daily winning trades where my little brother could not beat me. I made money. It might be different in your account but it makes sense that the following something works better than trying to anticipate and trade against it (when you should never do that).

Swing trading is in between and generally involving very few trades. I've noticed that swing trading sometimes takes a longer time than day trading due to the fact that you are not looking for explosive moves up or down, but a slow gradual move. But it can be done much quicker than forex if the market is volatile, so keep that in mind.

Here's where trend following comes in. Momentum begets more momentum, while range-bound markets are very hard to trade in the short term because there's nowhere to go but up or down when the range is too small.

Day trading is a versatile strategy that can be used to earn a profit without taking any risk. For example, traders can buy a stock and hold it for several weeks to months in order to collect dividends or sell short.

Swing traders are generally more risk-averse than day traders because they are not trying to capture small gains; instead, they aim at higher profits over longer time periods. Investors who are willing to take the time to learn how to swing trade from the start will likely be rewarded in the long term.

What You Will Discover in This Book

I am a straightforward guy, so you will find that I like to get right to the point. There will be no beating around the bush. I will not spout out terms at you like this is a textbook. All the words in this book are meant to be understood by a complete newbie.

Before we get to these explanations, one thing needs to be stated: day trading is a business. I will remind you that throughout this book, it's such an important thing to understand. Companies do not just spring up and become successful overnight, even though it sometimes appears that way to outsiders. Businesses take hours of devotion every day and months of behind-the-curtain work to become successful. In the case of day trading, it usually takes between 3 and 6 months of regular time and effort to get your feet firmly planted on the ground to see the results you want.

Trading is not a get-rich-quick scheme. If you do not have the time it takes to learn the business's ins and outs, this is not your career. In fact, you must commit the right amount of time, be able to handle a challenge or the excitement of an ever-changing career, and have the will to learn and grow.

It is possible to make money through all three of these strategies, but it takes practice and knowledge. If you like the idea of any of these three methods, it is important that you practice your trading strategy and learn more about technical analysis. Technical analysis involves examining past price behavior to predict future price movement.

With some determination and a lot of effort, you can be a successful trader in any of these fields.

This book will discuss these three strategies, and how they are related to one another.

Are you ready to be serious about gaining new tools and skills that will allow you to take control of your financial future? If so, then read on! I promise that this book will let you hit the ground running with day trading, even though you are starting with zero knowledge and experience.

Don't wait and miss out on the opportunity to take control of your finances and your life. Procrastination will keep you chained to financial slavery. Read this book in its entirety to see how YOU can be the master of your destiny!

We have a lot of ground to cover in a few pages. So, let's get started.

Chapter 1: Day Trading

What Is Day Trading?

The stock market is a vast place and there are millions of trades that take place all over the world, within a single day. There are both buyers and sellers in the market, and they will all have the same motive in mind; to increase their wealth potential.

Of all these trades, not everything will be of the same nature. Some will be long-term investments and some short. Long-term investments refer to those that are held for a long period of time. They are preferred by those who are not in a hurry to make money. Short-term investments, on the other hand, are those that are liquidated within a short period of time. They are not intended to be held for a long time, as owners will be interested in disposing of them early.

Short-term investments can be of many types based on the time that they are held. Some can be held for a month, some for a week, and some will be disposed of on the same day. This book will focus on the last option.

Better known as Intraday trading, day trading is one of the most preferred ways to trade in the stock market. Preferred mostly by those willing to part with their investment within a single day and realize a profit, or loss, from.

Intraday traders are interested in realizing a profit by capitalizing on the difference in the rates of these securities as opposed to long-term investors who will be in it for the Dividends.

Dos of Day Trading

Risk Capital

You have to understand that the stock market is a very volatile place, and anything can happen within a matter of a few seconds. You have to be prepared for anything that it throws at you. In order to prepare for it, you have to make use of risk capital. Risk capital refers to money that you are willing to risk. You have to convince yourself that even if you lose the money that you have invested, then it will not be a big deal for you. For that, you have to make use of your own money and not borrow from anyone, as you will start feeling guilty about investing it. Decide on a set number and invest it.

Research

Before you invest in the market, you need to research it thoroughly. Don't think you're going to learn as you go along. That is only possible if you at least know the basics. You have to remain interested in gathering information that is crucial for your investments, and it will only come about if you put in some hard work towards it. Nobody is asking you to stay up and go through thick texts books. All you have to do is go through books and websites and gather enough information to help you get started on the right foot.

Diversification

You have to stress diversification in your portfolio. You don't want all the money to go into the same place. Think of it as a way to increase your stock's potential. You have to choose different sectors and diverse stocks to invest in. you should also choose one of the different types of investments as they all contribute towards attaining a different result. Diversification is mostly seen as a tool to cut down on risk, and it is best that you not invest any more than 5% in any one of the securities.

Stop Loss

You have to understand the importance of a stop-loss mechanism. A stop-loss technique is used to safeguard an investment. Now say, for example, you invest $100 and buy shares priced at $5 each. You have to place a stop loss at around $4 in order to stop it from going down any further. Now you will wonder as to why you have to place the stop loss and undergo one. Well, by doing so, you will actually be saving your money to a large extent. You won't have to worry about the value slipping further down and can carry on with your trade.

Take a Loss

It's okay to have losses from time to time. Don't think of it as a big obstacle. You will have the opportunity to turn a loss into profit. You have to remain confident and invested. You can take a loss on a bad investment that was anyway not going your way. You can also take a loss on an investment that you think is a long hold and will not work for you in the short term. Taking a few losses is the only way in which you can learn to trade well in the market.

These form the different dos of the stock market that will help you with your intraday trades.

Don'ts of Day Trading

No Planning

Do not make the mistake of going about investing in the market without a plan in tow. You have to plan out the different things that you will do in the market and go about it the right way. This plan should include how much you will invest in the market, where you will invest, how you will go about it etc. No planning will translate to getting lost in the stock market, which is not a good sign for any investor.

Over Rely on Broker

You must never over rely on a broker. You have to make your own decisions and know what to do and when. The broker will not know whether an investment is good for you. He will only be bothered about his profits. If he is suggesting something, then you should do your own research before investing in the stock. The same extends to emails that you might receive through certain sources. These emails are spams and meant to dupe you. So, don't make the mistake of trusting everything that you read.

Message Boards

You have to not care about message boards. These will be available on the Internet and are mostly meant to help people gather information. But there will be pumpers and bashers present there. Pumpers will force people to buy a stock just to increase its value, and bashers will force people to sell all their stocks just because they want the value to go down. Both these types are risky, as they will abandon the investors just as soon as their motive is fulfilled. So, you have to be quite careful with it.

Calculate Wrong

Some people make the mistake of calculating wrong. They will not be adept at math and will end up with wrong figures. This is a potential danger to all those looking to increase their wealth potential. If you are not good at calculating, then download n app that will do it for you or carry a calculator around to do the correct calculations. The motive is to make the right calculations and increase your wealth potential.

Copy Strategies

Do not make the mistake of copying someone else's strategies. You have to come up with something that is your own and not borrowed from someone else. If you end up borrowing, then you will not be able to attain the desired results. You have to sit with your broker and come up with a custom strategy that you can employ and win big.

These form the different don'ts of the stock market that will help you keep troubles at bay.

Chapter 2: Conservative Strategy of Day Trading

Awareness Is Power

Monitoring chief exchanging measures isn't sufficient. Informal investors likewise need to screen and stay up with the most recent occasions and news on the securities exchange considering the monetary viewpoint, rate plans, and the Fed's revenue.

In this way, achieve your home assignment. Draw up a list of must-dos of the stocks you might want to exchange and be constantly kept insider savvy of the overall business sectors, and chose organizations. Monitor business news and search for solid monetary sources.

Put Aside Funds

Gauge how much cash you need to roll the dice for each exchange. Various everyday brokers lose under 1% to 2% in their exchange accounts. For example, on the off chance that you hold a $40,000 exchanging portfolio and decide to lose 0.5 percent of your cash for each arrangement, the potential trade misfortune is $200 (0.5 percent * $40,000).

The overflow measure of monetary assets ought to be saved to exchange. You ought to consistently be prepared to lose them. Remember, it could conceivably occur.

Put Aside Time, as well

Day exchanging takes as much time as is needed, so that is the reason its name is day exchanging. Indeed, you should spend the fundamental piece of your day on it. Try not to try and take a gander at it if you are limited on schedule.

The exchanging method needs a dealer for all time to monitor the current circumstance available and to gauge spot openings, which can seize any time inside exchanging hours. On-the-spot choices are the key.

Get Started with Small

As a beginner merchant, focus on a limit of 1-2 stocks over the span of a meeting. Observing and searching for promising circumstances are all the more effective with a couple of stocks. These days, it is amazingly unavoidable to realize how to exchange with fragmentary offers, so you can explain explicit, more modest dollar sums you need to contribute.

Avert Penny Stocks

Likely you are chasing at exchanges and low costs yet avoiding penny stocks. Often, these stocks are illiquid, and the opportunity to hit a bonanza is hopeless.

The greater part of the stocks, valued under $5 per share, are de-recorded from the significant financial exchanges and may just be traded absurdly (OTC). Stay far from these until you have a specific opportunity to take care of your job.

Time Those Trades

At the point when financial backers and brokers put in the requests, they begin to carry out when the business sectors open up in the first part of the day, which prompts the unpredictability of a cost. An accomplished player can settle on a satisfactory decision and perceive examples to make benefits. Notwithstanding, it tends to be better for novices to peruse the market without taking any actions for the initial 15 to 20 minutes.

Generally speaking, the center hours are less delicate. Accordingly, elements toward the end chime begin to go up once more. Albeit the times of heavy traffic guarantee openings, it's more secure for novices to deflect them interestingly.

Reduce Losses with Limited Orders

Tackle what sort of requests you will use to enter and leave exchanging. Is it accurate to say that you will utilize limit requests or market orders? At the point when you post a market request, it is executed at the most sensible cost available as of now—subsequently, the cost is ensured.

In the interim, a limited request guarantees the cost, however, not the execution. The restricted requests help you exchange all the more precisely, wherein you provide your cost estimate (not unreasonable but rather executable) for purchasing and selling too. More prepared informal investors may utilize alternatives techniques to ensure their positions as well.

Be Down-To-Earth Concerning Profit

To be worthwhile, a methodology doesn't have to win constantly. A ton of merchants just advantage 50-60% from their complete exchanges. Ensure that the danger for each exchange is restricted to a particular level of the record and that techniques for passage and exit are resolved and brought down unmistakably.

Keep Calm

There are events when the securities exchange evaluates your nerves. In the limit of an informal investor, you need to dominate the abilities to keep trepidation, eagerness, and expectation, under control. Your choices ought to be solemnly controlled by the presence of mind but not by feelings.

Adhere to the Plan

Prepared merchants need to act rapidly, yet not to think for quite a while. Why? Since they have a planned exchanging technique heretofore, close by the control to hold fast to that methodology. Following your recipe intently instead of attempting to seek after the benefits is additionally of an extraordinary significance. Try not to let your sentiments and feelings run over you, and put your arrangement away. Among informal investors, there's an expression: "Plan your exchange and exchange your arrangement."

We should consider a portion of the reasons why day exchanging can be so confounded before we jump into a portion of the intricate details of day exchanging.

Chapter 3: Advanced Strategy of Day Trading

When you are looking forward to capitalizing on the small frequent price movements, day trading strategies are the best for you. Any effective strategy that you will choose must be consistent and must rely on in-depth technical analysis that utilizes charts, market patterns, and price indicators predicting future price movements.

It is your responsibility to choose the most appropriate strategy that best fits your requirements. As a trader, it is good that you know the average daily trading volume.

Fallen Angel

A Fallen Angel is a strategy that involves a bond that has been reduced to junk bond status from an investment-grade rating as a result of the issuer's weakening financial conditions. In terms of stock, a fallen angel refers to a stock that has always been high and now has fallen considerably. Fallen angel bonds can be a sovereign, corporate, or municipal debt that a rating service has downgraded. The main reason for such downgrades could be attributed to revenue decline that generally jeopardizes the capabilities of issuers to servicing debt. The potential for downgrade often experiences a dramatic increase when expanding debts are combined with expanding debt levels. The securities of fallen angels are at times so attractive, particularly to contrarian investors who seek to capitalize on the potential. This enables the issuer to recover from the temporary setback.

Example:

Due to the ever-falling oil prices over several quarters, an oil company has reported sustained losses. The company, therefore, can decide to downgrade its investment-grade bonds to junk status as a result of the increasing risk of default. This will result in a decline in the prices of the company's bonds and, in addition, increase yields, which will make the contrarian investors to be attracted to the debt as they only see the low oil prices as a temporary condition. However, there are conditions where you are likely to go at a loss, especially when the fallen angel bond issuers do not recover. For example, if there is an introduction of superior products by a rival company, the issuers may fail to recover.

ABCD Pattern / Reverse ABCD Pattern

The ABCD pattern is a pattern that shows perfect harmony between price and time. ABCD pattern usually reflects the common and rhythmic style in the market movements. The geometric price/time pattern consists of three consecutive price trends with a leading indicator that can guide a trader to determine when and where to enter and exit a trade. As a trader, ABCD Pattern can be very important in identifying the available trading opportunities in any market (be it futures, forex, or stock) on any timeframe (be its position, intraday, or swing), and in any market condition (be it range-bound, bullish or bearish markets). Before placing a trade, ABCD Pattern can help you determine the reward and the risks of trade.

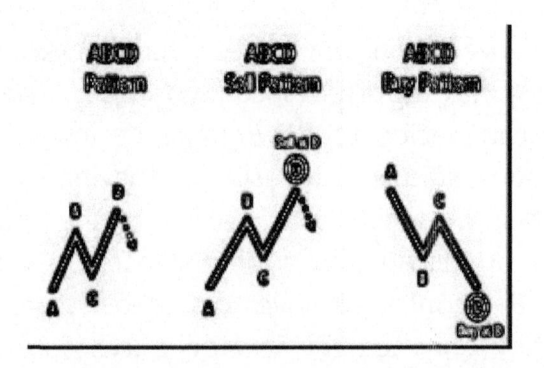

A representation of the ABCD Pattern (Above)

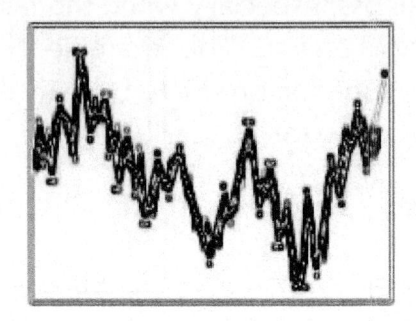

ABCD pattern on a trading chart

Bull Flag and Bear Flag

With technical analysis, a flag refers to a price pattern that can explode and move within a shorter timeframe to the prevailing price trend that has always been observed in longer time frames on a price chart. With the flag patterns, a trader can identify the possible prevailing trend that is continuing from a given point where the price has drifted against the same trend. Therefore, in the case that the trend resumes, by noticing the flag pattern, there will be a rapid price increase, and this makes the timing of a trade advantageous. Flags are areas of tight consolidation in price actions, and they show a counter-trend sharp directional movement in price. This pattern has 5 to 20 price bars.

Bullish Flag Formation

These are formation patterns observed in stocks that have a strong uptrend. Bull flags got their names from the fact that the pattern closely resembles a flag on a pole. A vertical rise in stock results in a pole, and a period of consolidation results in a flag. The flag is usually angled down away from the trend that is prevailing but also can be a horizontal rectangle. The bullish flag pattern starts with a strong price spike that is almost vertical. The prices then peaks and forms an orderly pullback where the lows and the highs become almost parallel to each other, making them almost form a tilted rectangle.

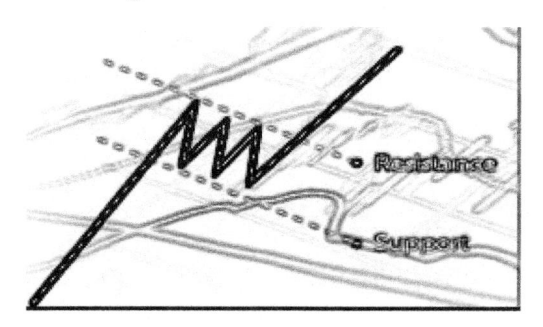

Bullish Flag Formation

The parallel diagonal nature is reflected by the plotted trend lines (both lower and upper trend lines). The breaking of the upper resistance trend line forms the first breakout. Another uptrend move and a breakout are formed when there is an explosion of the prices, causing prices to surge back towards the high of the formation.

Bearish Flag

The bearish flag is an inverted version of the bull flag. In this case, an almost vertical panic price drop is formed by the flagpole because the sellers make the bulls get blindsided and, as a result, there is a bounce having parallel lower and upper trend lines, forming the flag. The panic sellers are triggered when the lower trend lines break.

This flag is similar to the bull flag in that the severity of the drop on the flagpole will determine how the strength of the bear flag can be.

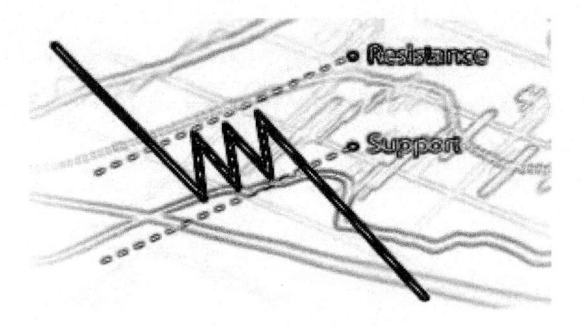

The Bearish flag

Develop Trading Skills

To become a trader, you are required to not only know about just finance or business but also hard science or mathematics. You must be an individual who can do deep research and analysis that can mirror the economic factors from a broader perspective, as well as the day-to-day chart patterns impacting different financial markets. As a trader, it is crucial that you need to sharpen your ability to concentrate and focus, especially in a fast-moving environment containing different people with different goals and ideas. You must also be able to practice self-control and regulate your emotions even when in situations upsetting you. Lastly, you should always be able to keep an accurate record of your trades to check on your account and to provide you with a learning opportunity that will help you become a better trader.

Chapter 4: Typical Beginner's Errors in Day Trading

ack of a Plan

While trading, it is important that you have a plan. A plan acts as a compass direction while trading; it shows you the move that you should take to ensure that it is a wise trade decision. In a plan, we have different goals while trading. Some of these goals make our investment in day trading worth our while. They give us hope to achieve more out of life and, at the same time, inspire us to push beyond our abilities. A person's failure to create a plan results in failure. You find that you make investments without properly evaluating all the underlying factors. In case there are some risks involved, you find that you are not aware of them. In turn, these risks exposed you to the possibility of encountering a loss. When such incidences occur, you are not well-prepared with risk management strategies since you failed to have a plan. It goes without saying that a plan will help you achieve a lot in the trading industry. Most of the time, it provides a bearing for the direction that one is taking while trading.

The biggest challenge comes when you are a beginner, and you do not know much about trading. At that point, it is very easy to make a mistake. Any slight move that you take matters and has a big impact on your future. A single move can either sabotage what you have built for years or make you stronger than you were before. We have seen people succeed at trading, and then, at one point, they lose all that they have worked hard to build. Your success in this industry is dependent on the plans that you have regarding your trading future. Any slight mistake will cause you to go down faster than you could climb up. As you trade, you may come to a point where you encounter a series of wins. Such incidences make you feel confident in trading, and, at some point, you may be deceived to think that you can easily achieve success. At that point, you may decide to do away with having a plan. Such simple decisions can make a huge change in your trading, and you end up making a loss that you may not be able to recover from.

Trading to Cover Up for Previous Losses

Most traders are victims of this strategy. After conducting your daily trades, things may not move as planned. You find that you might have expected to get a profit out of the trades made, but instead, you end up with a loss. To cover up for the losses, you decide to engage in another trade, hoping that things will be different. Contrary to your expectations, you end up encountering more losses than you would have imagined. It gets worse if you spent more money on that investment as compared to the previous investments. You get to a situation where you are full of regrets due to the wrong decision that you made. It is important to note that rushed decisions barely lead to anything good. In most cases, they end up in sabotage, and you may not be able to recover from some of these incidences. We ought to learn that two wrongs do not make a right. Once you have made a mistake, the first step does not involve bouncing back to the same thing that caused you to make a mistake. You need to calm down and identify where you went wrong and start reorganizing from that point.

At times, we keep trading even after we make losses because we are in denial. You find that you are in a phase where you find it difficult to admit that you can make a mistake. These difficulties, at times, arise due to the fact that we have high expectations. Anything that does not lead us to achieve the dreams we created for ourselves automatically makes us regret the decisions that we made. At that point, one becomes frustrated since things are not moving as planned. Instead of taking some time off to realize where you went wrong in the previous trade, you immediately engage in another without carefully thinking it through. This is perhaps one of the biggest mistakes that most traders make. While it is good to have big dreams and ambitions, it is important that you do not make wrong decisions while trying so hard to achieve some of these dreams. Well, since the whole point of investing is earning more from the investments that we make, it may not always be the case. Some days, we will encounter some losses, and they should not lead us in making rush decisions.

Overtrading

As a beginner, you may have started trading with huge expectations. You have this big dream of becoming an overnight success. You decide to invest heavily in your trades, especially after hearing what other traders are earning out of trading. Ideally, it is healthy to have self-belief and imagine that you, too, can get to the point that other investors have reached. While at it, it is essential that you have practical dreams that are achievable. Some people have managed to sell out the idea that trading is an easy task that can result in earning within minutes.

However, many people start trading and end up with huge frustrations when they fail to achieve their dreams as fast as experts. You find that with the excitement of engaging in trading, you end up engaging in multiple trades as a way to earn quick money. In this instance, most trade executions are not carefully planned; they are randomly selected. This means that you do not take time to come up with the right strategies to succeed in the different trades, and eventually, you end up losing.

At the same time, we have individuals who spread their risks across different trades. You are uncertain if you will end up making a loss or a profit. In this instance, you decide to spread your risks so that regardless of how the trade goes, you will not experience a total loss. In the beginning, this looks like an attractive strategy, and it almost feels like it is impossible to make a complete loss. However, you should remember that you are taking a gamble. This means that you can either earn a loss or a profit in both situations. It might occur that you experience a loss in all the investments that you made. In this case, that strategy will not benefit you in any way, especially since you still encounter a loss at the end. While coming up with the decision to conduct multiple trades, you need to be open to the idea that anything can happen. At the same time, you need to be well aware of the different option strategies that you can utilize while carrying out different trades. This allows you to remain focused and that you note some red flags before you end up making certain mistakes.

The Belief That a Big Investment Leads to Profits

Some people tend to have a misplaced belief that they need to make a big investment for them to earn a profit. This belief has caused a lot of individuals to make numerous mistakes while trading. We have had people invest a huge amount of their earnings, only to end up making a huge loss. For instance, you have $100 in your account, and you end up investing $90. With such an investment decision, you cannot afford to make a loss. Any wrong move can result in sabotage and make you lose what you worked so hard to get. At this point, with such an amount, you may end up feeling depressed after you have made a loss. Remaining with $10 can be challenging, especially considering that you had more, yet you lost it from making a trading mistake.

At this point, it is important that we learn to avoid placing all our eggs in one basket. In case of an accident, we may end up losing all the eggs and have none that is spared.

If you are a beginner, you should learn the importance of starting small. We find that most beginners are suffering from such decisions. You find that with the excitement of starting a new investment, you tend to overspend. This causes you to spend much of your time and energy on the new investment, and you barely take time to think things through. You end up making rash decisions that prove to be wrong later on, especially when things do not work in your favor. After experiencing a loss, you get to the point of self-realization that the move you took was wrong. We tend to have a misplaced perception that if we make a small investment, we equally receive small returns. Well, we have some trades that demand little from us and can result in huge incomes later on. We need to come to the point of understanding that the strategies that we utilize while trading can create a huge impact on our trading career. With a small investment and the right strategies, one can make a huge impact as they would make with a huge investment. At times, it all narrows down to the mentality that we have and uphold regarding different instances in life.

Ignoring the Expiry Date

Trades have a certain period where they are regarded as valid; after this period, the underlying stock becomes useless. You might have purchased some stocks and failed to be keen on the expiry date. Before you know it, you end up making a big loss after your stocks have been regarded as invalid. This is a sad way to lose the money that you have invested in your stock. To avoid being caught up in such, you need to watch the stock market carefully and make a move when it becomes favorable to you. This way, you avoid reaching the expiry date with nothing. To accomplish this, one way is to keep a record of your trades. If this is something that you keep referring to on a daily basis, it becomes difficult to overlook some of these things.

Lack of an Exit Plan

We are too fast in identifying the signals that lead us to engage in a certain trade, but we barely take time to identify when to exit a trade. This is a mistake that we end up regretting deeply. Mainly, if you engage in a trade, it is expected that you identify all the factors that can sabotage what you have built. At times, you find that one is in a position to earn a lot from a particular trade strategy. However, if they keep holding on to their position, they may encounter a loss. To avoid finding yourself in such situations, learn to note the signals that point out that you need to leave a given trade. Staying will make things worse, so exiting is the best solution at this point. At times, you might be betting on the possibility of making a huge profit or making a huge loss. In such times, you would rather exit the trade and earn a small profit than take the risk of staying. When you stay, you might not be sure if you will earn a huge profit or experience a huge loss.

All of the above are some of the key mistakes that the majority of us make while trading. However, if you feel like you are already making some of these mistakes, there should be no cause for alarm. I will provide some guidelines on how you can avoid making these mistakes while engaging in day trading options. There are more mistakes that traders make that have not been highlighted. You can learn more about them from other platforms. After all, as a trader, learning is something that you have to embrace.

Chapter 5: Swing Trading

What is the Swing Trading?

Swing trading is indeed a form of trading that seeks to grab short to medium returns on a stock (or another financial instrument) over even a span of weeks or months. Swing traders mainly utilize fundamental analysis to search for trading possibilities. In order to assess cost patterns and trends, these traders could use significant analysis.

Money Required for Swing Trading

Let's look at how large an account you'd like to swing a trade for livelihood.

If someone advises you that someone wants $X to sell for a livelihood, they wouldn't realize what they really are speaking about.

Several factors determine how long it costs to swing a trade for livelihood, so it isn't easy to have a total amount that would appeal to us.

Here are all the key topics to understand:

- The basic life expenditures
- The standard of lifestyle people chooses to sustain.
- Who else do people support?
- How much would you like to save per month?
- What other costs will you have incurred by investing full-time (hospital services, etc.)?
- The effectiveness and benefit of your trading strategy.

- How are you going to deal with a trade recession?

The smartest thing you could do is get a stable income when you're learning to exchange. Build your assets from the trading revenue.

Once you are ready to generate 2–3 times the existing trading revenue, you should try swing trading on a full-time basis. When it becomes clear that you're wasting funds by heading to work, it's definitely time to leave your work and trade. Or perhaps not.

It would be best if you still held your career and even served part-time to provide a stable income stream. It depends on one's priorities, what they are comfortable doing, and the other responsibilities.

The easiest way to start is to monitor your expenditures. Remember to implement any protection to deal with emergencies. Perhaps you might not notice how much you're investing.

On the other hand, you do not know how minimal your monthly expenses are. If that's the situation for you, perhaps it would be simpler to substitute your earnings with trading. Often, swing trading means keeping a stake either longer or shorter for far more than a trading day, but normally not longer than a few weeks and months. It is a generalized timeline since certain trades can last much longer than a few months, but the trader could also deem them swinging trades. Swing trades could also occur on the day of a trading session, but this is an unusual scenario that is caused by highly unpredictable circumstances.

The aim of swing trading is to catch a fraction of a possible market shift. Although some traders are looking for dynamic stocks with a lot of change, others might choose more subdued stocks. In any way, swing trading seems to be the method of determining where the investment's price is expected to move ahead, entering a spot, and then gaining a portion of profit if the move suddenly appears.

Efficient swing traders are indeed trying to catch a fraction of the anticipated market change, and then carry on to the next chance.

Often swing trader's measure trading on even risk or reward basic principle. By studying the map of the commodity, they decide where they would reach, where they could put an end to the loss, and afterward predict where they should make a benefit. If they lose $1 per stock on the setup that might fairly generate a $3 profit that is a reasonable risk to reward ratio. On the other hand, actually, losing $1 to raise $1 or just earn $0.75 is not quite as beneficial as that.

Swing traders mainly use fundamental analysis owing to a short-term habit of the exchange. That being said, a critical approach could be used to improve the analysis. For instance, when a swing trader perceives a constructive setup in a portfolio, they might like to check that the dynamics of the commodity are either favorable or strengthening.

Swing traders would also search for openings on regular charts and therefore will follow one hour or fifteen minutes charts to identify accurate admission, prevent loss, and take-for-profit amounts.

Swing Trade Strategies

Swing trader continues to search for multi-day graph trends. Many of the much more popular patterns include shifting average crossovers, triangles, cup-and-handle trends, flags, head and shoulder patterns. In relation to other markers, main reversal candlesticks could be used to develop a strong trading strategy.

At the end of the day, every swing trader formulates a scheme and tactic that brings them an advantage on certain trades. This includes searching for trading arrangements that aim to lead to stable fluctuations in the price of the commodity. It's not quick, and there's no technique or configuration that works every single time. With a desirable risk or reward, success is not expected at all times. The more amenable the risk to reward of a trading approach, the less necessary it is to succeed in order to generate net benefit over multiple trades.

The Real-World Example of the Apple's Swing Trade

The chart given above illustrates the time when Apple (AAPL) had a significant price increase. This was accompanied by the tiny cup and handle design that always signifies the continuity of the price increase if the stock shifts past the top of that handle.

In any case:

The price rises just above the handle, causing a potential purchase of about $192.70.

One potential stop-loss location is under the handle, labeled with a rectangle, close to $187.50. It typically depends on entry and the stop-loss, the approximate trading cost is $5.20 for each share ($193.70-$186.50).

If you are searching for a possible payoff that is at minimum double the potential risk, every price over $204.10 ($193.70 + ($2 * $5.20)) would offer this.

Apart from the risk to reward ratio, the trader may also use other escape strategies, such as that waiting for a fresh low price. For this approach, the exit sign was not provided until $226.46, when that price fell far below the previous pullback level. This will have ended in the profit of $24.76 for each share. Think of another way—12 percent benefit in return for much less than three percent uncertainty. This swing of trade consumed about two months.

Such escape approaches might be when a price is below the shifting average (never shown) or when the indicator, just as a stochastic oscillator, exceeds the signal point.

Pros and Cons

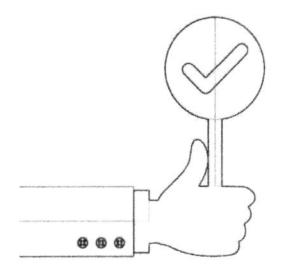

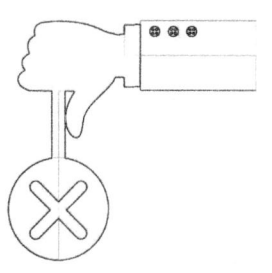

Swing traders typically keep a short to a long portfolio for at most a trading day but not longer than just a few days. This is a common time, but certain traders still prefer to keep positions indefinitely before their goal is met.

Swing trading is quite common with Forex retailers for two key factors. First, the Forex swing trade methods typically include entry and exit tactics that include a chart search just once or twice a day, and at most for some hours. This very flexible schedule is quite convenient for individuals with hectic lives and maximum work.

The core theory behind swing trading is to capture a bit of possible price fluctuation. Many swing traders favor higher-volatility assets (like foreign currency pairs), whereas others choose more stable market environments. In fact, swing involves purchasing lows and selling highs.

Anyhow, swing trading is mostly about forecasting the next market movement, getting into trading, and focusing on price movements. Productive traders aim to grab the only portion of the expected market shift and then search for another trading possibility. Another bonus of swing trading is that you do not have to waste the whole week in front of screens when the business lasts for hours or days.

This method of trading is very common among successful traders pursuing short and medium trading with the aid of various forms of research. Technical assessment is the most critical method of analysis that can be used in swing trading due to the comparatively short-term length of the transactions. In addition, the fundamental review should be carried out in order to allow an even clearer evaluation. Swing traders are normally looking for trading options on 4-hour and regular charts. Effective swing traders aim to make small trades over the span of one month.

Swing trading enables you to gain the benefit of the normal rise and fall of the Foreign exchange markets. Stock markets rarely move in one direction indefinitely, and by being eager to draw advantage of all that, you would maximize your gains when you theoretically make profits as the Forex price increases for the next several days and afterward make more as that market pulls down, which it would inevitably do eventually. You could find more openings by being in or out of markets. If you glance at every financial map, you could notice that there seems to be often a clear long-term pattern, but the stock will not necessarily be in the region of support or opposition. By getting in or out of the market in a couple of days, you will (usually) collect money and locate other established platforms for other transactions. This helps you propagate the uncertainty around and link up quite a bit less money instead of always trying to step up with the margin for the latest positions when you discover new trades. By ending your first spot, you won't need to deposit any funds into your savings to fund the second position.

Stop setbacks are usually less than long-term transactions. The limit loss on swing trading may be 110 pips depending on a four-hour chart, while the stop loss on the weekly chart, depending on an overall pattern, may tend to be 500 pips. This encourages you to put broader positions rather than relatively poor leveraged positions by long-term patterns.

You've got good limits. The swing trader is a much more complex trader and thus would usually have a particular region that they consider to be an indication that trading is going against them. That's why you understand precisely when the exchange doesn't work and can minimize the harm that poor trade could do. Longer-term traders typically have to lend themselves to the Forex market while they look for them all to "go for the fundamentals."

Some of the drawbacks of swing trading include that you will also get dragged down. That's because the market demonstrates support or opposition in a certain region, it does not guarantee that it will be rewarded today. Also, if you do a deal, you lose money. As a swing trader, you will have to take such risks quite often. You are likely to have setbacks periodically, regardless of how competitive you are. In the technical evaluation, you ought to be well-versed. It doesn't actually indicate "drawback," but it means hard effort. Usually, everyone can see the pattern on a chart that is moving from the bottom left to top right with time, so anybody attempting to swing the chart has to locate the entrances and exits. That is something that technical research could do, so you have to understand it first. This is time taking, it requires a unique mindset than long-term investing, with more ease. Although not generally scalping, swing traders face the risk of getting "startled out of stocks" when pullbacks in all of these narrower ranges tend to be much more aggressive than those staring at the weekly map. It is the psychological condition that several traders will inevitably have to struggle with throughout their careers.

Chapter 6: Conservative Strategy of Swing Trading

Keep it Simple

You may have heard of the term "paralysis by analysis." This happens when you analyze something to the point where you cannot make a decision. Some swing traders overcomplicate their analysis of security by using multiple indicators that all have to line up for them to enter a trade. In real life, everything does not often line up perfectly and you have to go with what you feel is right.

I have thus far covered many different tools and indicators you can use to help you to make a decision. You do not need to use all of them to be a successful swing trader. Once you find 1 or 2 that work well for you, you should then stick with those. If you decide to use a few different tools that all need to align, it will likely mean that you are not going to be trading very often. That is not necessarily a bad thing though. It is better to sit on your hands and wait for a good trade versus jumping in and out of marginal trade setups and slowly lose your money. The only one who wins, in that case, is your broker, as they collect fees for all of your trades (the successful ones and the losing one's).

Find several indicators that work well for you and focus on using them. Don't trade often, but trade smart, by knowing why you are entering a trade and, most importantly, knowing your risk to reward ratio and exit price points. As you gain more experience in swing trading, you will be able to better recognize trades that are going to work out even if everything is not perfectly aligned.

Having said this, when you do happen to find a number of indicators that are all aligned with the trade you are considering taking, it can certainly provide some level of confidence that you have a potentially profitable trade.

Treat your Swing Trading Activity Like a Serious Business

Should you decide that swing trading is a right fit for your personality, and that it is able to fit into your life along with all of your other interests and responsibilities, then you need to treat this activity as a very serious business. It will require an investment of time and effort, which hopefully will lead to some very good rewards.

Have a designated area where you do your research and keep all of your records. You are essentially becoming a professional money manager for yourself, so you should keep your work organized at all times. Everything you do with your business should be oriented toward making sure you are a success. If you feel like a professional, then you are more apt to trade like one.

Develop a Work Plan

Have a work plan and stick with it. Your work plan should include checking the market at the open and before the close. During this time, you should monitor your positions, set alerts and possibly enter orders at target levels that you think might get filled during the trading day.

I also recommend that you review your portfolio and market performance every night from Sunday to Thursday to ensure your assumptions about your positions and portfolio are still valid. On the weekend, you should try to do a more thorough review.

It is important to establish a work plan and keep it consistent. By keeping your work plan relatively consistent, you can measure your performance without introducing additional variables. Measuring your performance allows you to find areas to improve and make changes as you see fit.

Actively Manage Your Risk to Reward Ratio; Focus on the Entry

As a swing trader, your first and most important tool is your capital or cash. As I have said before, without cash, you cannot be a trader. I have written at length already about the necessity of assessing the risk to reward ratio on every trade and also on how much capital you should put into each trade. Following your rules on these points will prevent you from quickly losing all of your capital. You will be wrong on your trades some of the time and you need to make sure you live to trade another day.

Just planning and knowing your stop-loss and profitable exits are not enough for swing trading. Your entry becomes the next important step in your trade. You have already determined your stop-loss point and your target price(s) for a profitable exit. However, you calculated the risk to reward ratio based on an assumed entry price point.

Let's assume you found a good setup during a scan in the evening after the market has closed. The security closed the day at $10.50, and you see an upside to $12.00 with support at $10.00 where you would stop out. Therefore, you have a potential $0.50 loss compared to a $1.50 gain to the upside. That is a 1 to 3 risk to reward ratio, which is very good, and you are ready to pull the trigger and place a buy order in the morning. The market opens the next morning and the security you are ready to buy opens up at $11.00. What do you do? The novice trader is already invested mentally in the trade, so they buy. Unfortunately for them, their risk to reward is now 1 to 1, with the downside to $10.00 and upside to $12.00. This is no longer a good trade at that entry point.

The rational trader reassesses the situation. They may put a buy order in at $10.50, hoping to catch the entry they wanted on the security during the normal daily price gyrations in the market. This will give them the risk to reward ratio that they need to make a good swing trade. If they do not get a fill, then they need to reassess again, and maybe move on to finding another trade with a more appropriate risk to reward ratio.

The bottom line, do not get emotional and chase a trade. The "fear of missing out" can motivate you to make a bad trade and you should be aware of this when picking your entry price on a trade.

Measure Your Results and Adjust Accordingly

As a trader, you must track your results to measure your performance. Nothing gets improved that does not get measured first. Every trader should use a tool to record the different aspects of each trade, from initial assessment through to the risk to reward expected, the entry point, and, finally, the exit. The tool can be a spreadsheet, it can be done on paper or it can be web-based. It does not matter how you do it as long as the process allows you to track the details of each trade as well as your performance.

Once you have your trades recorded in detail, you can go back at any time and review how the trade worked. You can compare your performance using the different indicators, i.e., is one working particularly well versus the others you use? Are you getting good entry points on your trades or do you need to exercise more patience? Are your exits working or are you consistently exiting a trade too early and not getting all of the money you could on a profitable trade? Are you respecting your stops?

Having all of this information to review will help you adjust your trading process and plan accordingly to maximize your performance without letting emotion enter into your decision-making.

Chapter 7: Advanced Strategy of Swing Trading

To become a perfect trader using the swing style, the major thing you need to know is how to identify any potential trade. When you have identified such trade, you can now begin to apply the various concepts that we have covered so far in this book. The steps we have given here are simply to show you how to apply all concepts you have learned so far. You can easily use some of these approaches to quickly execute and identify trade as well as direct potential traders to the techniques.

Sizing Up the Market

Any swing trader should definitely know more or less about the market; to be a complete trader, you should know about the currency market, state of equity, fixed income, etc. You need this because hardly will you find any market that is not related. So, if there is an increase in the prices of a currency, you should expect that there will be a bear market in the case of bond prices. There will almost be an immediate flaw in equity if the bond price keeps falling rapidly. Commodity prices go up if the dollar weakens. We can continue to show how all these things are related.

The main thing is that you will be able to improve your trading ability when you look at all these major markets; this will allow you to be able to predict the possible directions of any other market.

Identifying the Top Industries

There are numerous ways you can use to identify the leading industries. You can use the top 10 % list to identify the stocks on the long side of the market. You can make use of the High Growth Stock Investor (HGS Investor) software which is a better tool than focusing only on the top 10 %.

Ensure that you look out for swing trades that are promising in the industry group within the top 10 % for long candidates and the short candidates' lower 10 %. Doing this will make you know the leading group and you can easily select from the candidates within the top two industries.

Selecting Promising Candidates

Many traders opt for technical analysis when they are selecting promising candidates but it will be better to use the fundamental analysis first; this will facilitate easy selection of your promising candidate. Then, you can now use technical analysis to time your entries and exits.

- Screen securities: When you screen security, you are sure to have filtered out penny stocks and thinly traded securities. We recommend you use the format below to screen

Market capitalization ≥ $ 250 million
Average daily volume ≥ 100,000 shares
Stock price ≥ $ 5

- Access chart patterns and rank the filtered securities: You can easily rank filtered securities using the price to cash flow ratio or earnings rank. After that, you can access the charts of promising stocks.

Determining Position Size

Now that you may have found your trade, you may be having problems with allocating it. You will know by now that we recommend that you set your position by risk level rather than by percent of capital, this will easily allow you to get your position size through knowing your stop loss, and limiting losses level should usually be between 0.25 % and 2.0 % of the value of your account in case the security comes to the level of the stop losses.

Executing Your Order

Ensure that your swing trading time commitment is in consistency with your order entry. If you are a part-time swing trader, you can enter near the closing price by using the limit orders at the exact day the signal was generated. Full-time traders can buy at a better price if they add the intraday trading overlay.

It is important that you enter a stop-loss order as soon as you execute your trade whether you are a full-time or part-time trader, except you are a full-time trader who tries to watch your position during market hours every day.

Recording Your Table

Recording of your table should follow the execution of your trade. The recording serves to keep your journal up-to-date and you can easily find some helpful details there. This book has dealt with the information that your journal should contain. Ensure that you keep such information simple and always strike a balance so that you do not enter too much irrelevant detail.

Monitoring the Motion of Shares and Exiting at the Right Time

When you might have recorded your positioning in your journal, you should be keen on monitoring them and ponder on your best exciting strategy. We recommend that you use the following scenario to know when exactly to exit.

- When you see the position meandering sideways.
- When you notice that the position is unprofitable.
- When the position is profitable.

Enhancing Your Swing Trading Skill

We may have given you some insights into trading but keep in mind that no trading system works efficiently 100 % at every time, likewise, you cannot be 100 % perfect as a swing trader. Expect to lose but know the numbers of losses you can accommodate. One of the ways by which you can become an efficient trader is that you should try as much as possible to evaluate your journal every month; this will make you able to easily detect your winning and losing pattern of position.

You can then alter your trading pattern based on the winning or losing position, but do not change this often because of one or two losses that you may eventually work upon. If you lose hugely, then it is possible that you will not need to adjust your entry and exit strategy but rather your risk management strategy.

Chapter 8: Typical Beginner's Errors in Swing Trading

Mistakes are always part of the game in any trade. Traders in swing trading also make mistakes that cause them to fail. Others commit mistakes due to ignorance of the different rules and strategies used in swing trading. This is all about giving details of the various mistakes committed by the different traders in swing trading.

Below are the various mistakes swing traders commit while trading:

Lacking a Trading Plan

Most of the traders starting off on swing trading lack a well-defined plan. What do you normally think of when you do this? Swing trading is a risky arena. You need to be well-armed and prepared before entering into trading. Lacking a proper trading plan makes you misbehave in your trading, which is a very bad idea.

You normally lack a trading routine when you fail to have a plan. You find yourself lacking the objectives and goals for your trading. A trading plan enables you to stick to the plan and work hard for your objectives. Failing to have a plan makes you do things when you feel like it is so risky in the swing trading environment.

A plan is basically composed of objectives and strategies. Without it, it is like going to a war with no weapons with you. Prepare yourself with a good plan to be able to know the risks involved in the market since it enables you to formulate your own trading strategies.

Lacking a Time Horizon for Your Trading

Always known as a swing trader the duration you have for investment reasons. It enables you to be aware of the time duration you have before expiry. When you select your time horizon to be until retirement, it tells that you have to invest for a while before the time of retirement.

Failing to Utilize the Stop-Loss Orders

Stop-loss orders are very crucial for all kinds of traders. You need to implement it for safety reasons during trading. A trader who fails to utilize stop-loss orders strategies ends up with huge losses on their trading. You find yourself making big losses that could be controlled.

Losses all times turn down the success of any business. Failing to arm yourself so well in trading is just a total failure for your swing trading. You need to be alert with the crucial strategies in swing trading so as to survive and succeed.

Lacking Control over the Trading Losses

Losses will normally occur in most businesses, but does that mean you should have no control over them? You need to make fast and efficient actions when losses occur in your swing trading, even the smaller losses. Ignoring the smaller losses will make them accumulate so hard, and time will reach you will have no control over them.

You need to be serious about the losses that come up and be able to handle them before they shut down, you're trading. Losses promote no growth in swing trading. You need to have policies with you on how to handle losses. Most of the traders neglect this mistake which makes them fail in swing trading tremendously.

Putting Much Trust in Financial News

Watching and following up on news is not a bad thing, however, you need to be extra careful with what you hear or come across online. Some bloggers mislead novice traders a lot on how to handle their trading. You should be alert with all the information. Some people just want to see fail. Do not apply all the information you hear from other people. Have your own ways of how to handle things in swing trading. You do not need to copy what others are doing, people have different abilities. Rely only on the trusted sources and swing trading forums. Consult the experts in swing trading for any information that you have heard and you are not sure about it. Have trust in yourself that your ways will also succeed in swing trading.

Working on Too Many Markets at Once

A high number of swing traders fail in their trading due to being over-occupied with too many markets at once. You are not like a robot machine; you need to decide on a reasonable number of markets that you can handle. Do not be greedy for money, you need to calm down and at least focus on a few and perfect your skills rather than being involved with too many markets.

This will make you get out of control. Concentrating on many markets is even not healthy for your body and mind.

You do need to select every market. You should choose the ones you are highly interested in, perfect your skills on them, and ace swing trading.

Being Overconfident

Being a confident swing trader is a good thing, but being extra than that is really a poor thing to do. Overconfidence has killed the dream of many swing traders. Traders are normally over certain with what they are doing and fail to list down even the risks that may be involved in their trading. You need to remember both the worst-case and the best-case scenarios in swing trading while planning. Consult others when you need help with your strategies, you may learn a few things that will help you in your trading. Do not be that kind of a bold trader who does things alone with no trainer or some sort of master in swing trading. Do not trust yourself that much, you might be doing things the wrong way.

Lack of Patience

Good things take time. This saying is also relevant in our case here. Most traders have no patience at all with the huge profits. They only want money to be accumulated in the first days after joining swing trading. That is not possible unless all you want to accumulate are huge losses. You need to give yourself more time before you begin to earn more money.

The kind of traders who rush in trading for their greed for money end up nowhere. You need to be realistic sometimes to succeed in swing trading. Do not rush the trade, the money will keep coming. Do the right thing at the right speed. Do not implement too many strategies in your trading and get confused. Work with at least one successful trading strategy and relax.

Indiscipline

It is not advisable to be undisciplined in swing trading. Success is directly related to discipline. When you are disciplined in your trading, you are able to handle your trade with caution and with the right mindset. Traders who mix their trading procedures and activities with other things end up mixing everything up. You need to be aware of all of your strategies and objectives at your fingertips to be able to know what you want to achieve. Not being disciplined makes you even forget your targets and your policies. This, of course, leads to total failure in your trading.

Too Much Focus on Profit

Profit-making is one of the main objectives of all businesses, but why focus too much on profit and forget about other crucial factors in swing trading? Factors like risk management and loss handling losses also need attention. Do not be the kind of traders who just think of making a profit and end up making big losses in their trading.

You need to have a balance on how you handle your trading activities. Do not allow to accumulate high profits which have the same amount as losses. There will no earn since the losses made will decline both your trading capital and your profits.

Failing to Trust Your Abilities

You need to have trust in your capabilities. As a beginner, you should not compare yourself with the expert successful traders. This will make your esteem to decline. You need to be yourself and remind yourself that you will succeed. All you need to do is to comply with the strategies and objectives that you wrote down. You also need to learn a lot and do much research in swing trading in order to succeed.

Using Much Money on the Investment

The amount of money you are dedicating for investment should be a good amount of your disposable income that you can quickly or easily refund. Utilize a little money at the beginning to avoid huge losses. The higher the amount of money you use for swing trading, the higher the number of losses that can come up due to the many risks that are involved in swing trading. Most traders boast around with a huge amount of cash for trading and, unfortunately, end up making huge losses. Also, do not trade with your school fees or rent, you will have issues with your school finance.

Being Emotional on the Money Lost

Catching feelings in trading is not advised for any swing traders. Some traders give up when losses occur and decide to quit. Do not be a faint-hearted trader; you need to be strong that the money lost will get refunded. Stand strong and wish yourself good luck.

Being Too Much Aggressive

Most unsuccessful swing traders failed to succeed because of their aggressive behavior. Being aggressive makes you lose a lot of money which leads to the failure of swing trading. This normally happens on a bullish type of market. Relax, and everything will work out.

Laziness and Being Irresponsible

All types of trading are tough. You need to put much effort into your swing trading in order to widen your knowledge. Failing to do much research will not keep you informed and updated. You need to go with the trend. Do not be left behind. Failing to go through different newsfeeds on swing trading will enable you to be outdated.

Irresponsible swing traders who lack trading plans and strategies get confused and finally decide to quit swing trading. You need to be responsible and make decisions even during the worst-case scenarios. Do not fail to work even on the small losses that occur during swing trading. Trade responsibly, taking into account all the risks involved in swing trading.

Ignoring Risk Management Trading Strategies

What do you expect when you fail to implement the few strategies needed for risk management? Swing traders who fail to implement the risk management strategies of course end up being involved with too many risks. You need to check on the different swing trading strategies that exist and choose the best that handles risks in swing trading.

This will protect your trading capital and also the amount of profit accumulated. Failing to arm yourself well enough will bring failure to your trading.

Implementing Many Small Moves

This mistake is normally committed by novice traders who make moves on any small changes in the market. You find yourself making trades even on your weakest points. There are high chances of big losses during this time. You need to be extra cautious and only make sure moves when relevant changes occur in the market. Small moves contribute to huge losses. Trade at the right time according to your trading plan. Avoid this mistake in order to succeed in swing trading.

Being so Close to the Market

Traders who focus so much on the swing trading market end up living in worries all the time. You end up putting much effort even on small things that need less attention. Do something else other than trading. You can even do some cooking or even water flowers. Give yourself some time to catch a breath with a good mindset that everything will work out well. Do not be so close to the market—you will worry too much for nothing.

Lacking a Swing Trading Strategy

Strategies are like guidelines that exist in swing trading to help you when making decisions. Most of the swing traders forget to formulate the trading strategies when formulating the swing trading plan. Lacking swing trading strategies is a very bad idea. Strategies help you in managing risks and accumulating more profit. Always stick to your working strategies that are according to your trading plan.

Chapter 9: Forex Trading

Forex is commonly known as foreign exchange or FX, and it involves the buying and selling of different currencies with the aim of making profits based on the changes in the value. The forex market is the largest market in the world; it is larger than the stock exchange market. Therefore, it attracts many traders. There is high liquidity in the foreign exchange market, and as such, this attracts both experienced and beginner traders. In fact, the forex trade market is so large that all the stock markets in the world cannot match its capacity. The foreign exchange market is decentralized across the globe; therefore, all the different currencies in the world are traded freely.

Currency Pairs

There are very many types of currencies across the world, and all of them have three-letter symbols; for example, the Euros are EUR, American Dollars are USD, British Pounds are GBP, Swiss Francs are CHF, etcetera. The currencies have been majorly divided into two major and minor currencies. The major currencies involve these derived from the powerful economies in the world that are; the USA, the UK, Japan, the Eurozone, Australia, Canada, New Zealand, and Switzerland. These currencies create forex pairs with each other and with other minor currencies.

When one goes to a store to purchase some groceries or any other item, he/she needs to exchange one asset of value for another, for instance, milk for money. This applies to forex exchange too; buying and selling one currency for another. Every pair involves two currencies whereby one buys or sells the currencies against the other.

Forex pairs can be classified into three types, namely Major pairs, Exotic pairs, and Minor pairs. The major pairs always consist of the United States Dollar, and many people trade in them. The major pairs are USDCHF, USDJPY, EURUSD, AUDUSD, GBPUSD, NZDUSD, and USDCAD. The minor pairs involve all the currencies participating in the major pairs apart from the United States Dollar. They include CHFJPY, EURGBP, EURAUD, JPYAUD, NZDCAD et cetera. The exotic pairs involve one minor currency and one major currency, for instance, USDNOK, USDKSH, EURTRY, and so on.

How Does Forex Work?

Just like the stock markets, one can trade currencies depending on his/her prediction on the changes of value. The greatest difference between stocks and currency trades is that forex can trade down and up very easily. If one thinks that a particular currency will have a value increase, he/she may buy it, and if he thinks that the currency will fall, he/she may sell it. The forex market is so large that finding a buyer or seller is too easy compared to other trade markets. Let's assume that a trader hears reports that a country such as China will devalue its currency with the intention of drawing more foreign investors into the country. If he/she thinks that the devaluing trend will continue, the trader may sell the currency of China against another, for example, the USD. The more the currency of China devalues against the United States dollar, the higher the trader's profit. However, if the currency gains value against the US dollar, then the trader will have increased losses and may want to leave the trade as soon as possible.

Summarily, Forex trading involves placing a bet on the value of one currency against the other. Remember that in a pair, the first currency is the base while the second currency is the secondary or the counter. For example, in the EUR/USD the EUR is the base while the USD is the counter. If a trader clicks buy or sell, he/she is buying or selling the base. This means that if a forex trader thinks that the EUR will increase in value in contrast with the United States dollar, he/she will buy the EURUSD. If the trader thinks that it will drop, he/she will sell the EURUSD. If, for instance, the asking price 0.7060 and the bid price is 0.7064, and then the spread price is 4 pips. Whether the value of the EUR rises or falls, the trader will make a profit or loss once he covers the spread price. The spread price is usually higher for minor currencies.

Basic Terms in Foreign Exchange

In foreign exchange, the term 'Position' refers to a trade that is in progress, and it is basically classified according to the expectation of traders. The term 'long position' refers to the trade where the trader has purchased a particular Currency (the first in a pair) with the expectation that the value will rise. When the trader sells back the currency to the market (expected to be a higher price than the purchase price), the trade is complete, and the long position is "closed." A short position refers to the trade where a trader sells a currency (the first in a pair) with the expectation that the value will fall, and then he/she buys it back at a lower price. When the trader buys the currency back ideally for less than he/she sold it the trade is complete, therefore "closed."

The pair that is mainly traded in the forex market is the American dollar versus the Euro or USDEUR. The currency identified on the left side is referred to as the base currency, while the one on the right is referred to as secondary currency. The base currency is the one a buyer or seller wishes to buy or sell, while the second currency is the one a trader uses to make the transaction. Each trade pair has two prices, the bid and the buy. The 'bid' is the selling price of the base currency, while the 'ask' is the buying price. The difference between the bid and the asking price is referred to as the spread, and it indicates the amount that brokers charge to keep the position open. The spreads become narrower when more currency is traded when a currency has high volatility. If a pair is very rare, the spread will be wider.

Usually, the quote prices are presented with 4 numbers after the dot. In the case of EURUSD for example, the price might be 1.2589 to mean that for every Euro that a trader wishes to buy, he/she will have to put in 1.2589 US dollars. Changes occurring in the value of the currency will be seen on the last figure after the dot. It is mainly referred to as a pip. The gains, the losses, and the spreads will normally be indicated in pips.

Another term commonly used in forex trading is going long, which means buying and going short means selling. A bullish trader normally predicts that the market will rise, while the bearish trader hopes that the market will fall to benefit. The term bull market indicates that the market will rise or increase, while the bear market indicates that the market will fall or decrease. Experienced traders normally base their decisions and strategies on market trends; therefore, they follow all the relevant events within the markets. The study of trends helps the traders to gain profit in the market.

Formally, traders had to call the brokers and inform them of the actions he/she should take in the market. However, technology has made it possible for many traders to transact directly using software referred to as a trading platform. There are many trading platforms available for the internet, computers and even phones. Every trader selects a platform that will work well with his/her trade strategy to reap maximum benefits.

Leveraged trading, also referred to as trading on the margin is a process that allows the traders to hold larger positions than they can with their own fortune only. In a large number of forex pairs, a trader can hold maximum leverage of 400:1, which means that for every $400 the trader will invest $1. Consequently, if he/she wishes to purchase 100000 EURUSD at the price of 1.2674, instead of paying $126,740 he/she will pay 25 percent for the amount. One should remember that the losses and profits usually depend on the size of the position, and as much as leveraging trade can magnify the profits, it can also enhance losses.

Example: Let's say a trader wants to transact in the forex market. He/she logs onto the trading platform and checks the bid and ask price. Assuming that he/she finds that the asking price is 1.2356 and the bid price is 1.2359; the pip will be 1.2356-1.2359= 3 pips. The three pips will go to brokers. If for instance, that trader believes that the Euro will rise, he will put a 'buy' command. He will then select a particular number of units he/she wishes to buy for instance 10,000. The normal price for that would be $12356, and if the trader is relying on leverage trading, he will pay $30.89. If the markets move up as the trader had indicated, say to $1.2360, then he/she will make a profit.

Chapter 10: Conservative Strategy for Forex Trading

Analysis-Based Trading Strategies

Technical Analysis

As the name suggests, 'analysis,' this method focuses primarily on the evaluation of the market trends through charts as a means of predicting the to-be price trends of the market.

In this method, an evaluation of assets is done basing on statistics and past analysis of market actions like the then volumes and the past prices.

Technical analysis is not done with a primary objective of weighing the underlying value of assets; instead, charts with other measuring tools are used to define the patterns that are helpful in the future forecast in market actions.

It is believed that the market's future performance is easily determined by the past trends in its performance.

Trend Trading

In technical analysis, a trend is a very critical aspect. The tools used in this type of analysis, have a common motive which is simply to determine trends of the market. Therefore, to trend is to move; in this context, it means the way the market is moving.

As we know, the fore market is a wavy and zigzag motion that represents the successive trails that define clearly troughs and peaks which are sometimes called lows and highs?

Depending on the available trends of the lows and highs, a trader can define the nature of the market type.

Other than the popular notion of the highs and lows, there is yet another format of the trends in Forex trading called: uptrend/downtrend and sideways trend.

Support and Resistance

It is quite imperative to know the meaning of the horizontal level before defining the support and resistance strategy. This is the level in the price signifying market support of the resistance. In technical analysis, resistance and support as used to refer to the lows or highs in prices in that order.

Support, in this case, refers to an area on a chart, which shows that the interest in buying is stronger than the selling force.

This is revealed through successive troughs. On the other hand, resistance level, as represented on the chart refers to an area where the buying force is outweighed by the selling concern.

Range Trading

It is also referred to as channel trading. This signifies the absence of market direction that may be associated with a lack of trends. It is used to identify the movement in the prices of currencies within the channels of which it is tasked to establish the range in the movements.

It can be achieved by linking sets of lows and highs to the horizontal-trend line. This is to say that the trader is tasked to establish the resistance and support levels with the area in the middle, which we refer to as the trading range.

Technical Indicators

When we talk of the technical indicators about Forex trade, we simply refer to the calculations that are inclined to the volume and the price of a given security.

When used, they are meant to corroborate quality and trend in the chart patterns as well as enable traders to identify sell and buy signals altogether. These indicators in technical analysis can create sell and buy signals via divergence as well as crossovers.

Whenever the prices go across the moving average, crossovers are seen however, divergence occurs only if the indicator and the price trends both move in different and opposite directions implying that there is a weakening in the price trend.

Forex Charts

In Technical analysis, we refer to a chart as a representation of the shifts in prices within a given time frame graphically. It reveals the movement in the security price over some time.

Different charts can be applied in search of diversified information and the skills and knowledge of the researcher.

Forex Volume

Forex volume indicates the total securities by number, traded in a certain time interval. The higher the volume, the higher the level of pressure; this is as indicated by chart specialists.

They can easily define the downward or the upward shifts in volume by observing the volume bars on the lower side of the charts. When a price movement is accompanied by a high volume, it becomes more valuable than if it is accompanied by low volumes.

Multiple Time-Frame Analysis

Security prices must be tracked over a period and in a unique time frame. This is so because a security price will tend to go through a series of time frames, and therefore, analysts need to review several time frames so that they establish the security's trade cycle.

Trading-Style Based Strategies

This is yet another technique, which offers a different way of classifying the trading styles. Through trading styles, trading strategies can be created, which could include but not limited to a buy-and-hold strategy, portfolio trading, trading algorithm, order and carry trades,

It is entirely dependent on your level of understanding, power, and weaknesses that determine the strategies that you will apply. Everyone needs a trading strategy, which best suits his desires according to his ability to apply it.

There is not a style of trading that you must use if you choose to trade, because what suits a person does not suit you and your needs.

Day Trading

This is the act of holding a position and disposing of it the same day. This implies that this type of person does not hold security for more than a day.

You have the right if only you have the ability to conducting more than one type of trade in a single day as long as you do not hold a position for more than one day. This means that before the closure of the market, you must have liquidated all your open positions.

There is a challenge in today's trading where if you hold onto a position for that long the chances of losing it are high. Based on whatever style you are using, the targets in the price may vary.

Scalping Strategy

This is characterized by short and quick operations and is applied mainly to achieve vast returns on small price variations. Scalpers can initiate over 200 trades per day with the intention of making good profits on small shifts in price levels.

Fading Strategy

In this case, fading refers to a trade that is initiated against the trend. When the trend moves up, faders sell in the hope that there will be a fall in prices; similarly, they may buy when prices rise.

They buy when the price is escalating and sell when the prices are coming down a notion called fading. It is very contrary to other trends and also to the nature of business.

The trade is usually against the usual trends with reasons such as the buyers at hand may be risking. The securities are usually over-purchased and the earlier may be set for profits.

Daily-Pivot Trading

Currencies are very volatile, and as such, traders may wish to capitalize on that to make profits. This is exactly the case with the pivot strategy.

A turning point, as well as the pivot, is a very critical and unique pointer obtained through the computation of the statistical average of the low, high, and closing prices of currency pairs.

The secret to this strategy lies in the aspect of purchasing securities at their lowest prices and selling them at their best prices in the course of the day.

Momentum Strategy

This is characterized by defining the strongest position that will end up trading the highest. In this case, the trader may drop the currency with signs of dropping in price and go for that currency that has positive signs of going up through the day.

A momentum trader has got several indicators, which help him detect the trends in the securities before he makes his decisions called 'momentum-oscillators.' Such a trader will tend to invest deeply in news feeds which he entirely depends on for price predetermination and decision making.

Buy & Hold Strategy

In this case, a position is bought and held for quite a long before being sold so that the prices escalate even if it takes longer. Whoever does this has no business with the short-term price changes as well as indications. However, this type of strategy best suits the stock traders.

In this case, technical analysis becomes invalid because the trader here is a passive investor who has no rush in determining the market trends of the stocks and securities.

Order-Types Trading Strategies

Trading in order will help the trader to join or move out of a position at the very right time by use of various orders, which include but not limited to market, pending limit, stop-loss, and stop as well as other orders.

At this particular moment, most advanced platforms are fitted with different kinds of orders for trading that are not the common buy/sell buttons. Every order type signifies a certain strategy. You must know how and perhaps when to handle orders before you can use them effectively.

The following are trader orders that can be applied by traders:

- Market order- is put to enable the trader to buy/sell at a ripe price.
- Pending order-enable traders to buy/sell at previously set prices.
- Limit order guides the trader to buy/sell assets at specific price levels.
- Stop-loss order placed to lower a trade risk.

Algorithmic Based Strategy

This is as well-referred to as 'automated' Forex trade. There is software designed to help in the predetermination of times for purchasing and selling securities. This software operates on signals draw from the technical analysis.

To trade in this strategy, you need to issue instructions over the kind of signals that you would wish to search for and its subsequent interpretation. This is an example of a high trading platform, which comes with other supportive platforms for trading.

Examples of these kinds of trading platforms include meta-Trade 4 and Net-TradeX. However, Net-TradeX is a trading platform in which, in addition to its normal functionalities, it presents automated trading through its advisors.

This is referred to as a secondary platform that yields automatic trading and further sophisticates its processes through a language called: "Net-TradeX language."

It goes ahead to provide room for some trading operations traditionally, for example; to open and to close a position to place orders as well as the use of the technical tools for analysis purposes.

Meta-Trader 4 similarly is a trading platform, which makes it possible for the execution of algorithmic trade via an incorporated program-language "MQL4." In this type of platform, traders can come up with called-Advisors, trading–robots with indicators of their own. All acts of making advisors, which include: to debug, to test, to optimize and compiling the program, are all done and made active through the meta-Trader 4 editor.

Robots are made in this case to take away the emotional concept of the traders, which in most cases hinders the free and competent engagement in the trade across the platforms. Emotions have and supply a negative attitude to the traders, especially when there is hope for a loss.

Chapter 11: Advanced Strategy for Forex Trading

How to Create Your Easy Strategies to Start and Make Money?

There are two different types of people who trade on foreign exchange. 1.) Those who have chosen to make a full-time career of it, and 2.) Those who prefer to dabble enough to make a tidy little passive income. The strategies listed here are for those part-time traders and are simple and practical enough to help you get started earning in a short amount of time. Here are the strategies that you may not have even thought about when it comes to trade, such as different currency pairs, the time of day you trade, and additional features you can take advantage of to help you on your way to success.

The Variables to Watch Out for

The new trader should always approach their first investments with caution. You should know the currencies you want to trade and the time of day you plan to make your transactions. We will talk about why this is important a little later. It is also good to develop a plan to make sure you are ready to trade simultaneously every day. Consistency is the key to success. By now, you should have at least a basic understanding of how to read market data and read the price action charts. If not, go back and study those again before you proceed. You should also have a good grasp of the market's function and the different currency pairs and know how to make the best use of the technology available to help you.

There may be many things to think about, but it is possible to make a nice steady income in the Forex Market as a part-time trader. However, as your income rises, it may be tempting to cast your day job aside for this type of income, but I advise you to wait for a while before making such a major decision.

Let's Talk About Time

There is a reason why timing is critical when you invest in foreign exchange. While the market is open 24-hours a day, the trade opportunities will change throughout. Find the time of day when most individuals will be making similar trades like the ones you plan to make. Keep in mind that if you plan to trade only on occasion, the opportunities to buy or sell a particular currency will be reduced. In a volatile market like Forex, rapid changes can frequently happen, so when you know the kind of trade you want and when it is most likely to be done, you can take great pains to be on point when the most activity is likely to happen.

Those who choose to trade at night may find that only certain types of currencies are available at the volume sizes you need. By learning how volume trades are made, you can choose from the currencies available when actively working on the market.

The foreign markets are open 24-hours a day because as the day passes through certain time zones, individual markets have definite open and close times. When the business day closes in a one-time zone, it will be open in another. It does not mean that all markets are open 24-

hours a day. This is important to understand when choosing to trade currencies.

For example, the trading day starts in the Asian time zone at 8:00 AM (21:00 GMT). Later, the areas in Australia and Tokyo followed by Singapore. Some of these areas will be open simultaneously, at least for a few hours each day, as they move around the globe. As the one-time zone closes, another will open with a few zones overlapping each other throughout the day. It is this overlap that can create a lot of excitement in the market. As a trader, this can provide you with many great opportunities and many risks throughout the day.

One of the best strategies is to become very knowledgeable about the times and how each zone relates to the other. As you analyze the market, you will eventually be able to single out how other traders navigate these time changes and adapt their forms of trade accordingly.

Other Factors Related to Time

Other factors may not readily come to mind when it comes to trading on the Forex Market. Daylight Savings Time and other time factors can create whole new challenges for your trading practices. Holidays can cause changes in opening and closing times all around the globe. As you study the currencies and the things that affect their trade, you will also need to understand how these factors can impact the type of trades made and when they are made.

You can see how this can have an impact on your trading practices. For example, if you plan to trade the USD/JPY currency pair, you need to know what times those trades are available. A quick look at these markets' schedules to learn when the time zones overlap will tell you when you will make those trades. A Google search reveals these times for the US markets:

The New York Exchange is open from 8:00 AM – 5:00 PM EST.
The Tokyo Exchange is open from 7:00 PM – 4:00 AM EST.

As you can see, these times do not overlap anywhere on the clock. But since it is not enough to settle for a good time to trade, you want to find the optimum time to make the trade. In most cases, you would wait for the overlapping time to trade these two currencies, as this will be when a business is the most active. So, what can you do here?

The solution is simple. The currency pairs see a lot of activity around the clock. Almost every nation with currency in the system will be trading in these two currencies. The yen is actively traded globally, and so is the US dollar. Because they are both very stable currencies, you will see lots of activity for these two throughout the day. So, when considering the timing for this type of trade study, the market to find the most active trade times to make your purchase.

You can learn this by consulting the hourly volatility chart that shows exactly how many PIPs the USD/JPY moves per hour. The times to avoid trade will be straightforward to spot once you understand what you are looking for. As a general rule, the slower the currency movement, the less likely an investor will see a positive change.

Other currencies traded against the USD that could pose a time challenge are USD/EUR, EUR/GBP, EUR/CHF, and EUR/JPY. Of course, many other currency pairs can also present similar challenges, but these are the most highly traded, which increases your chances of making a profit. As you can see, Forex strategy starts with knowing how to take advantage of the time to maximize your profits. The secret is to trade during peak times, where high volumes are being traded to ensure liquidity. Since each currency pair has its own times of peak performance, getting in at the right time takes on a whole new meaning.

Chapter 12: Typical Beginner's Errors in Forex Trading

Overtrading

Overtrading simply refers to a situation where you trade for longer hours than expected, or you invest more money than you should. We have already mentioned that Forex trading can be addictive, like most gambling games. If you get into Forex without having a clear understanding, you may end up making the mistake of overtrading. When can overtrading occur most likely?

When you are making too much money: It is common for traders to keep on investing in a trade as long as they are making money. The right time to stop trading is when you are making enough money. People who are addicted to trading do not get enough of the action. They continue trading even after reaching their profit target for the day, week, or month. For such people, profits do not mean the end of the business. They keep on investing and trying to earn more even if they have made enough profit, risking losing the money they have already made.

If you are on a winning streak, as we said before about the anti-martingale technique, it could be okay to increase your risk and continue investing. But, first of all, you must understand this technique. Then you must include it in your trading plan with written rules; you must test it, and above all, you must follow it also during losing streaks of trades. Most of the time, traders act this way not because they are following a trading plan, but because they are following their greed.

To ensure that you avoid overtrading, you need to set your trading hours. Forex is a 24-hour business. This means that you can trade at any time of the day at any place you are. To avoid the temptation to continue trading even when you are tired, set your trading hours. You should also ensure that your trading hours occur at a time when you are free. Most people who overtrade combine their trading with other activities. If you continue trading at a time when you should be busy doing another activity, you may find that the combination of multiple activities takes away your ability to trade properly due to the lack of focus.

When you are making losses: The other scenario where people get involved in overtrading is when they are making losses. Losses are very enticing. It is dangerous for a person to start making losses when there is still a lot of money in his or her trading account. For instance, if you funded your USD with $10,000 and set your investment risk at 2%, you may think that your investments are insignificant. In this case, after losing the first $200, you may think that you can recoup your money. While it is okay to try to recover lost money, you should not rely on impulse and emotions when making such critical trade decisions. Your impulse will tell you to reinvest immediately. Most people invest huge sums of money in the hope that they can recoup their money in the shortest time possible. The more money you lose, the more confused you get. Your mind loses control, and you eventually start making choices that are not rational.

This overtrading mistake can be avoided if you take a break. After closing a trade, whether it leads to profit or loss, you should take some time away from the screen. This is a matter of discipline. You should make up your mind to ensure that you control your actions and make trade decisions that will positively impact your life. You must learn to accept and deal with losses since they are part of the business.

When you have too much time: The other reason why people engage in overtrading is that they have too much time on their hands. They say, "An idle mind is the devil's workshop." While Forex trading is a good and positive venture that can earn you a handsome amount of money, you should not spend your entire day thinking about the trade. As we have observed, Forex markets operate 24 hours a day. You may be fooled to think that trading around the clock is the best option for you. In reality, you should avoid trading for long hours. Even if you have plenty of time on your hands, you should try as much as possible to stick to your chosen trading hours. Engage in other activities after trading, even if it means playing games or watching movies. If you notice that you are getting addicted to your Forex trading apps, uninstall all trading apps on your mobile devices so that you may stay away from the trading platform when it is not the right time to trade.

When you lack self-discipline: The other reason why most traders get involved in overtrading is simply a lack of self-discipline. If you know you are a person who lacks self-control, try avoiding Forex as much as possible. Self-discipline simply means that you have patience and emotional control. You should be able to stop yourself from taking emotional actions. The only way to survive as a Forex trader is to ensure that you follow the rules you have outlined in your trading plan. There is no way you can expect to succeed if you cannot follow the rules, you have created yourself. People who lack self-control are quick to make decisions without considering the consequences. Forex trading is a game of numbers. In this trade, you must be sure that every action you take has the maximum potential of being a success. If you start making decisions that are not based on facts, you may end up losing a fortune in Forex. As you learn to trade, you eventually stop making errors that are associated with emotional instability. Your discipline will help you stop overtrading or making any other mistakes that you might have committed. To ensure that you stop overtrading, you must first answer the question of "How much trading is too much trading?" Once you know your limits, try to stop when you reach them.

Canceling the Stop Loss and Allow Losses to Run

This is a mistake that is made by both young and experienced traders. The stop-loss order is one of the most important tools that you can use to manage your risk in your trading activities. Unfortunately, the stop-loss order also limits your profits in some instances. You may feel that the price is just about to reach a resistance or support level, but the stop loss point has almost been surpassed. What most traders do is to cancel the stop-loss order and stay in, hoping that the trade may turn in their favor.

If you cancel the stop-loss order, you may result in two situations: you can make a lot of money or lose a lot of money. The fact that you can make a lot of money should never be a motivation for you to cancel the stop-loss order.

Canceling the stop-loss order is a big mistake because if you follow a strategy with a statistical edge, probabilities are in favor of the stop loss, not vice versa. Any action you take in Forex should be geared towards protecting your capital and then providing an additional income. If you approach Forex with the mentality of getting rich quickly, you will likely lose all your money.

There are two main reasons why people end up canceling their stop-loss orders:

A chance to make more profits: As already mentioned above, Forex trading does not guarantee 100% success even if you follow all the outlined strategies in this book. With an estimated success rate of 50%-60% based on analytical data, most traders try making a lot of money in a short time by choosing an alternative means of prediction. This means that most traders are more likely to use their instinct than follow a strategy with a statistical edge. While instinct trading can be beneficial, it is also very risky. If you keep on reading volatile news and blogs, you may fool yourself to think that you are ready for the Big Money. Those who encourage traders to make bold moves are experienced brokers. They encourage you to stop following your plan and take risks based on how you feel. Our first rule of thumb is always to ensure that emotions are not part of the business. If you spot an opportunity that you feel can lead to huge profits, avoid it as quickly as possible. What you feel does not matter when it comes to real numbers. If the charts are giving you a negative signal, it is because the odds are against your trade. Instead of trying to win against statistics, it is better to turn to more secure options. The best security option you have is the stop-loss order. With the stop-loss order, you can change the way you do your business and protect yourself from the risk of losing all your money.

Fear of Losing: The other reason why any person would cancel the stop-loss order is the fear of losing. If you are a wise trader, you understand that one position does not determine your final outcome. Trading is a probability game. What really counts is that on a large number of trades, the profits outweigh the losses. Losses are part of the game, and you have to learn to accept them. If one position turns out to be negative, you have the chance of trading in a new position and making more money. The main reason why people should protect their principal investment using the stop-loss order is that they can still engage in other trades and keep staying in business. Being in a position to continue trading even when things have gone against you is the best thing that can happen to any trader.

Not Following the Trading Plan

The other big mistake that is made by almost all traders is failing to follow the trading plan. The main reason why traders should follow the plan is that it helps avoid making mistakes. Mistakes are caused by bad choices, and bad choices cause losses. If you are in a moment of frustration, you are likely to make a mistake. However, if you stick to your trading plan, you do not give your emotions the chance to lead you to lose money. Some of the common errors that occur due to abandoning the trading plan include:

Changing your trading strategy: One of the most important factors outlined in your trading plan is the trading strategy. We have looked at multiple strategies. Each of the strategies has its positives and negatives. When you create a plan, you choose whether to use one strategy or use many. The choice to use a certain strategy is determined by your understanding of the market and your trial results. Before you settle on a trading strategy, it is advisable indeed to try it out and find if it is effective according to your market analysis and if it gives you a statistical edge. Changing your chosen trading strategy midway is the worst mistake you could make. This is not only a mistake because it may lead to losses, but it leads to questioning your full trading plan. The only reason you have a plan is so that you may follow it and utilize it to the end. If you believe in whatever you are doing, there are chances that you will make money from it. In case you choose to change the strategy, it should be because you have observed the market and analyzed it. Change your trading strategy only if you have the data to show that it is better to do so. You should have valid reasons, which can be verified by other traders.

Conclusion

So, what do you think?

How long did you get through this little book? Was the duration enough to help you ease into your new life as a day trader?

If that is the case, then wonderful! Hopefully, the book has provided you with the assistance you need to navigate this new and challenging world.

While I was writing this, I sometimes talked to my friend Ron about how this was turning out to be an encapsulation of everything that I have learned in day trading. While I read textbooks, mingled in online forums, and attended little certification classes, it is a friend's guidance that got me through everything. I am very thankful that I have a friend in him.

But guess what? He likes being in the background, happy that he is successful, at least with the goals that he has set for himself. As for his mentee, yours truly, day trading has afforded me something that goes beyond the usual 9 to 5. I get the excitement of wins and the obvious benefits of earning extra money. It felt liberating to be outside my cubicle prison, at least in spirit. I had been able to extend my reach to something that could help me earn money without me toiling for hours a day.

So why did I say that success was earned, mainly because I had trading friends?

Well, think of it this way.

A stranger approaches you and tells you about this new way of earning money. He wants to have a nice chat over coffee. This stranger insists that you have to invest at least $25,000 so that you can trade with a reputable broker.

Nothing he said is wrong so far. Aren't those the facts that we have talked about?

But he is a stranger. The coffee invite sounds reminiscent of some scammers that you know of.

With Ron, it is different. He did not invite me at all. Instead, he just got engrossed in day trading. Then, his life changes followed. He left his 9 to 5 to set up his business. We got worried about him because he was a married man with kids. He could not just be leaving something that is so sure?

What about pension plans? Retirement? Security?

Suddenly, we saw that life had started to improve. We were the ones who asked questions, and he was ready to answer.

What I am trying to say here is that I hope I was able to answer your questions. I hope that you were able to consider me as your day trading guide, your Ron. Indeed, I am not physically present. However, I wish the contents of this book would have given you a sense of security to find a reputable broker to day trade with.

Are you still in your 9 to 5 cubicle? It does not matter. Nobody is rushing you to do anything right now. It is our decision to make. Right now, though, you have been equipped with everything that you need to succeed:

    Chapter 17.   Knowledge

Chapter 18.   Opportunity
Chapter 19.   Assurance

You now know-how:

- To find the right broker
- To identify a good trading platform
- To read and understand the various parts of a trading platform
- To recognize market trends and patterns
- To apply risk management
- To make decisions with or without a mentor
- To play it safe while also being decisive
- To handle stress in the short-period trading format
- To see the science and logic of trading

When to use Day Trading?

Day trading is best for people who are comfortable taking a lot of risks. You need to be able to cope with high amounts of volatility and be able to trade during all hours since day trading is an active style of investing.

Day trading is best suited for short-term traders who follow the markets closely and can take advantage of intra-day price changes.

When to use Swing Trading?

Swing traders typically have more time on their hands than day traders, which means they can either wait hours or days for the market conditions that they want. Unlike day traders, who try to make a few quick trades every day, swing traders might hold their stocks for weeks or months at a time.

If you're interested in market timing, developing a good sense for when price levels will be low or high helps to have the time to wait for the conditions to develop.

Swing trading is best suited for long-term traders who follow the markets. Swing traders like to buy stocks and hold them for up to six months at a time, selling them only if they show signs of deteriorating performance.

When to use Forex Trading?

The world's currency markets are huge and can move dramatically. If you believe that moves in currency rates will significantly affect your portfolio value, you might want to try forex trading.

Forex trading requires more experience and knowledge than the other options on this list, so it's less suitable for people who only have a little bit of experience. If you choose the forex market, you'll need to be able to read charts and technical analysis to figure out trends and pounce on opportunities as soon as they appear.

Trading strategies are especially important in the forex market because it doesn't have an open-ended period of trading. For example, if you want to buy foreign currency at 1:00 today (when rates are high) and sell at 1:00 tomorrow (when rates are low), you stand to make a tidy profit if rates stay relatively flat between those two times.

The markets are open five days a week on average, with some high-volume currencies trading for 22 hours per day. Some currency pairs are only open for a few hours per day, so intraday opportunities might be limited.

Forex trading is best suited for people who have experience in other markets or in trading in general. If you want to trade forex, it's probably best to start developing your skills through practice accounts and classes. You might not be able to afford big losses (or profits) at first, but the more you trade, the better you'll get at it and the better your chances of success.

You are ready. You did not even have to leave the comfort of your home. This book has provided you with a path that will help you journey towards financial success.

Be wary, though. This book does not promise miracles. It only assures you that no matter how seemingly volatile the financial market is, you can make sense of patterns and trends to win at it.

For now, I wish you the best of luck. I hope you will make the most of the information that you have been given. Remember that your patience, strategy, and risk management are more crucial to success than high-tech monitors and computers.

BONUS NFT & METAVERSE

Here you will find the complete book

Please scan the QR code and download the free version of the book in PDF format from the website

Printed in Great Britain
by Amazon